The Road to Yale

ISBN: 1545066558
ISBN-13: 978-1545066553

Editors

Jennifer Lu, Sharon Li, Grace Li, Lynn Han, Wendy Peng, and Shixia Huang

Authors

Alex, Charlie, Emma, Eric, Jared, Jonathon, Katie, Kayla, Lourdes, Nini, Olivia, Sato, Sophia, Steven, and Vivian

Project Managers

Shixia Huang, Wendy Peng, Julia Guo, and Jason Huang

Cover image and design: Jennifer Lu

The Road to Yale

Application, Essays, and Résumés that Wowed Yale Admission Officers

Yale Admitted Students

Table of Contents

THE ROAD TO YALE

Introduction

College admissions, and the stress, test prep, hard work, and sheer hope that come with it, can be an arcane and mysterious journey. On one side, talented and dedicated high school seniors write essays and submit applications into the great void of the online application. On the other end are acceptances, but what happens in the middle?

Beneath all the numbers is one unflagging consistency—the students.

It's easy to think of college applications (and acceptances) as random chance, but the fact of the matter is that top-tier schools more often than not want many of the same people. It's not a smooth bell curve—it's skewed, a lopsided balance where some students are accepted to every college they apply to, from their state school to the Ivies, and some aren't so lucky.

This book is about those that were lucky—about those that were more than lucky. This book is about you.

Everyone you will read about was accepted to Yale. Why Yale? Because Yale is incredible and challenging beyond all imagination, and we want to share our college applications with other students who share the determination and hope that we all had. In reading *The Road to Yale*, you will see that all students come to Yale through their own unique ways. Whether they're driven by music, community service, or research, passion is the defining trait of Yale students. We all spent high school—and the years before—pursuing our passions, despite many challenges, and Yale offers us the opportunity to keep doing so. It is a pleasure, and a privilege, and it's the reason we want to help you get here, too.

If you're already writing your college applications, *The Road to Yale* may help you discover just the right way to present yourself. If you're just getting started with high school, this book may help you find activities to try, summer programs to consider, and opportunities to keep in mind for the future.

If you're searching for a book on how to get an easy acceptance, you can stop reading. There's nothing easy about this. From the second you decide you want to achieve something to the breathless moment right before you submit your Common Application, the road before you is made up of hard work and unflagging determination.

In these pages, you'll read about what we did, but more importantly, you'll read about who we are.

We hope to see you soon.

Editors' Remarks

All the application materials and essays in *The Road to Yale* are printed as they were submitted, although names and locations have been altered for privacy. Since the essays have not been edited (and we asked that our authors not edit them retroactively), you may discover errors. It is our intention that readers see these for themselves. We urge you to proofread your applications carefully and to seek second readers before submitting. However, if you do miss something, know that it happens to others, too. Take a deep breath—it'll be okay.

It is worth reminding our readers not to plagiarize essays, sentences, or short answers from this book. *The Road to Yale* is intended to serve as inspiration for readers. College applicants must write their own essays and original answers. Plagiarism is considered academic dishonesty.

THE ROAD TO YALE

Chapter

1

College Preparation Timeline

College Preparation Timeline
Grace Li

BEFORE SEVENTH GRADE: EXPLORATION

- Develop strong reading and writing skills, which will help you in your academics, college applications, and in all of your pursuits.
- Explore different activites, read up on the subjects that interest you, and don't be afraid to try out unfamiliar things.
- Get involved in school activities such as math and science clubs, afterschool art and writing programs, and more.
- Participate in sports.
- Learn an instrument.
- Volunteer for local organizations and school community service efforts. Discover the causes you are passionate about, and commit to helping them in the ways you are able.
- Participate in talent searches. Look into your school district's gifted and talented programs and participate in national programs such as the Duke Talent Identification Program, Johns Hopkins Center for Talented Youth, Northwestern University's Center for Talent Development, and Davidson Young Scholars. Talent searches usually require achievement tests (the ACT/SAT tests) or IQ tests (i.e. Stanford-Binet Intelligence Scales).

Big Picture

It's never too early to begin exploring and discovering your interests. Try out different activities, sports, and extracurriculars, and don't be afraid to pursue the activities that you love!

SEVENTH AND EIGHTH GRADE: PREPARATION

- Keep exploring!
- If you have discovered 1-3 causes and subjects you are passionate about, dedicate yourself to spending more time and effort on them.
- Hone your leadership skills by designing your own community service projects (e.g. musicians can organize a benefit concert, or actors can direct a play at a nursing home).
- Foster your creativity, and don't be afraid of showing it to the world. Submit art and writing pieces to local and national competitions.

One well-known competition is the Scholastic Art & Writing Awards (www.artandwriting.org), which accepts submissions from seventh-graders and up.

- For serious athletes, focus on one sport and aim to qualify for the high school team.
- For advanced students, consider taking classes at the local high school for an additional challenge.
- Familiarize yourself with your high school requirements. Many high schools have a weighted grade point system: AP and Honors classes are weighted more heavily than regular classes, which affects GPA and class rank. For example, the first year of a foreign language in high school (e.g. Spanish I or French I) may be weighted as a regular 4.0 class, while the second-level language classes is weighted as a 6.0. In that case, you could take the first year in eighth grade and then take the second-level language class as a freshman. Understanding high school requirements allows for strategic planning.
- Participate in talent searches. Take the SAT or ACT in seventh grade. With a qualifying SAT or ACT score, you can participate in gifted programs, such as summer courses at Duke TIP and Johns Hopkins CTY, and you can apply for the Davidson Young Scholars program. Students are also usually invited to participate in gifted programs through their school districts based on their standardized test scores, though qualified students may also register online to participate in the talent search.

Big Picture

These are the years right before you start high school, so you should spend this time preparing for high school and making sure you know what to expect when freshman year comes. By getting involved in music, sports, or other activities early on, you can develop your interests and get a head start. This is also important in terms of academics: taking classes early or learning ahead will make high school a lot easier.

Summer Before Freshman Year

Enjoy your summer vacation, and consider taking classes or credit by exam in order to take more advanced classes in high school. Summer camps are also a good choice, which can help develop leadership abilities, athletic talents, or other skills.

FRESHMAN YEAR: JUMPING IN

- Choose courses strategically. Make sure your course selection is the best for your interests and your ability.
- Manage your academics responsibly. Keep up with all homework and take every assignment seriously, even if it's small. If you experience any problems, meet with your teachers or counselor as soon as possible and ask for help.
- By the end of your first semester, you will have an idea of where you are academically and can set goals accordingly.
- Get to know your teachers by raising your hand in class, contributing to discussions, and asking questions.
- Meet with your high school counselor and talk over a plan for your classes over these four years. A good relationship with your counselor means a strong recommendation letter, but more importantly, counselors know a lot about the school and are wonderful to talk to and get advice from.
- Check out your school's clubs and join the ones you're interested in (it varies by school, but 3-6 are a reasonable number). Become an invested member: get to know your fellow members and club leaders. If there is something you're interested in but your school does not have a club, start thinking of how to start one, i.e. talking to a teacher who could sponsor it, finding out whether other people would be interested, etc.
- Build your leadership skills by leading projects in clubs and becoming involved in activities outside of school, such as taking on more responsibilities in volunteer work and community service.
- Participate in competitions in your area of interest. Some suggestions: Scholastic Art & Writing Awards, the American Mathematics Competitions, and science Olympiads in fields such as biology, chemistry, physics, and computer science.
- Create an Excel spreadsheet to track your activities and hours spent. You will need this for college applications senior year.
- Create a résumé. Compile all of your personal achievements in one place: debate tournament awards, sport championships, piano competitions, state-qualifiers for academic teams, etc.

Big Picture

Although it may feel overwhelming, everything matters right now, from your grades to your extracurricular activities. But don't worry—colleges know that freshman year is a big change, so your job is to make sure that you don't take on more than you can handle. Join a few clubs, get involved in service and academic competitions, work hard in school, and you'll be on the right track.

Summer Before Sophomore Year

Find a camp, summer job, or volunteer work. Even if you can't pursue a volunteer or community service project full time, find ways to incorporate it into your day-to-day or family life.

SOPHOMORE YEAR: CONTINUATION

- Take challenging classes. Work hard to achieve the best grades you can in all of them.
- Meet with your counselor to review and revise your high school plan. Update your counselor on your summer activities and what you are passionate about—your counselor should be building a full idea of who you are and what you care about.
- Take on officer positions in clubs.
- Lead larger-scale volunteering projects, both in school or out of school.
- Continue attending academic competitions and aim to go further than you did last year, e.g. making semifinalist in an Olympiad, advancing to NFL Nationals for debate, etc.
- Prepare for the SAT and PSAT by taking practice tests and think about when you want to take the SAT (everyone is required to take the PSAT at the same time junior year, but the SAT can be taken anytime). Research the ACT to see if that option is better for you.
- Think about which SAT subject tests you want to take (many schools require two, while some schools have more specific subject requirements). It's best to take the SAT subject test right after the class about the subject, e.g. take the Math SAT II after taking pre-calculus, and the Chemistry SAT II close to the AP Chemistry test, so the material is fresh on your mind.
- Study hard for AP tests, and aim for all 5s! Remember that doing well on AP tests not only looks good on college apps, but also gives

you college credit and allows you to take higher level classes once in college.

- Maintain your activity spreadsheet and add more information to your résumé. Take time to reflect on and adjust your activities. Focus on your strengths and pursue your passions.
- Find scholarships or competitive programs to apply to, and ask your teachers and counselor for recommendations. During this process, you'll practice application writing and learn to work with teachers and your counselor to obtain strong recommendation letters.

Big Picture
This is a busy time, but the main point of this year is to continue doing well. Take on more leadership roles and be more active in clubs, sports, and other activities. A few awards definitely don't hurt, and be sure to add on to your résumé as you go. And, as always, foster a good relationship with your teachers and counselor.

Summer Before Junior Year
Find an opportunity in an area of interest and pursue it, whether through summer programs, internships, or in your personal time. For those interested in science, find research programs geared towards high school students, or reach out to professors at nearby universities to ask if they are willing to take on a high school student. Other options are volunteering at a hospital, working in a law office, or interning at a congressional office. No matter what you do, whether it's an internship or a summer job, give it your all—even if the job isn't in an area you'll continue pursuing, it is important to develop positive relationships with your supervisors and mentors for the future.

JUNIOR YEAR: THE VITAL YEAR

- Study, study, study! Take the most challenging courseload that you can balance. Look into what it takes to be an AP Scholar with Distinction and a National AP Scholar.
- Prepare for the PSAT. Each state has a cut-off score. If your PSAT score is at or above your state's cut-off score, then you qualify to be a National Merit Semifinalist. From there, you will fill out an application for National Merit Scholar.
- Prepare for the SAT over the summer and plan when you will take it during the school year. It's perfectly fine to take it a second time to achieve your dream score.
- Make sure you get to know your teachers this year! Almost all recommendation letters are written by teachers you have in your junior year—you're more mature than you were sophomore year, and you will have known them longer than your senior year teachers, who will only have you for a few months before college apps are due. Ask teachers for recommendation letters before the end of the summer if you already know who you are going to ask.
- Meet with your high school counselor again, and go over the last two years and your goals. Give your counselor a résumé and discuss college applications in the fall.
- Ideally, you want to have one or more major leadership positions at this point, whether it is National Honor Society president/officer or debate captain or student government.
- Continue volunteering and leading projects regularly.
- Aim to reach the state or national level in academic or athletic competitions.
- Continue maintaining your activities spreadsheet and résumé. Take the time to reflect on and adjust your activities, especially as you begin taking on more senior leadership roles in organizations.

Big Picture

In many ways, this is the most important year in terms of preparing for college. You will be taking challenging classes, working to excel at the state or national level, and leading clubs and volunteer projects. Manage your workload carefully, and be both ambitious and realistic about what you can handle. It's better to devote your energy to excelling in a few areas than to burn out by juggling a dozen activities for the sake of padding your application. Remember to keep up good relationships with your teachers and counselor, maintain your grades, and prepare well for all of the standardized tests you have to take (PSAT, SAT/ACT, and SAT Subject tests).

Summer Before Senior Year

Apply for competitive programs in your area of interest, using the experience you gained last summer as a springboard. For scientific research programs, consider Research Science Institute, the Simons Summer Research Fellowship, Garcia Research Scholars, Summer Science Program, and others. You can find more programs by looking at the résumés in this book or by looking online. These programs are selective, so don't worry if you are not accepted. No matter what you end up doing this summer, make the most of the opportunity by giving it your all. Now is the time to start building bridges with future peers, colleagues, and supervisors, who will be more than happy to give you a glowing reference or serve as a mentor if you can build strong relationship with them.

This summer, you should also begin assembling your college application. This is also your last chance to study for the SAT if you would like to improve your score further (there is an October test date, but you will not be able to see your score before it is sent to your early action/decision colleges). Start writing your essays and ask trusted friends and family for feedback. Revise, revise, revise. Start filling out your application forms as early as possible. Your Excel spreadsheet and résumé will come in handy! Decide whether you want to apply early to a school, and if your application is a good fit for applying early.

SENIOR YEAR: FINISHING TOUCHES

- Ask teachers for recommendation letters as soon as school starts, if you haven't done so already. It's important to do this early, in order to give your teachers as much time as possible to write them. Inform them of all the deadlines, and politely check in with them along the way.
- Start your Common Application, also as early as possible. The earlier you start, the more time you have to edit your essays and make sure your application is in the best shape possible.
- Talk to your counselor. You need two recommendation letters from teachers and one from your counselor, so let your counselor know your plan for college applications and ask for the recommendation

letter if you haven't already.

- If interested, submit your research to Siemens, Intel STS, or the Google Science Fair. You can also apply to some of these in junior year.
- Apply for the Coca-Cola Scholars Program, and any other scholarships you find. The deadlines range, so putting them all in your calendar is a good idea. Recommendation letters are also needed for these, and you should tell your teachers about all the things you need recommendation letters for at the same time.
- Make sure you are keeping up your grades and still taking challenging classes. You are required to submit a list of classes you are taking senior year if you apply early action/decision, and if you apply in the regular round your first semester grades will be on your transcript.
- Submit your application! You will hear back in mid-December for early action and late March for regular.
- Even after submitting your application, you may want to continue maintaining your activity spreadsheet and résumé. You may need to update colleges for your new achievements and awards, especially if you are deferred or waitlisted by your dream school.

Big Picture

This year, the focus is on college applications. Make sure you are keeping up your grades and staying involved in extracurricular activities (and maintaining volunteer work and leadership positions), but much of your time will be spent on preparing your application. Remember that your teachers are working hard at this time too (they have a lot of recommendation letters to write), so be sure to thank them when everything is done. Show your appreciation with a thoughtful thank you card—not just for writing you a recommendation, but also for their important roles in your education! Your parents have also worked very hard, so be sure to thank them too. And celebrate when you finish—you did it!

Summer Before College

Enjoy your summer!

Chapter

2

Why Yale

Why Yale?
Sharon Li

Ten months and nine days ago, I wrote a one-hundred word paragraph titled *Why Yale*. Ten months and nine days ago, I was learning through a computer screen about the world that is now my life. And now I am writing this essay once again—putting myself back in the shoes of that nervous seventeen-year-old who first fell in love with Yale.

Yale is my home away from home, and even when consumed with work, being here means finding solace in an incredible community. It's the good with the bad, it's seeing thirty tour groups a day but knowing you were one of them just a few short months ago—back when you were walking through Old Campus surrounded by students playing spike ball, walking (hiking) up Science Hill, taking in the breathtaking architecture and wondering how this is possibly a college and not a 1,015-acre museum.

Yale is beautiful. Yale is taking classes in Battel Chapel and getting lost in the splendor of the chandeliers and organs and stained glass windowpanes and the intricacy of the ceiling (possibly while you're supposed to be learning about the rise of mental asylums in the mid 1900s). Yale is studying in Sterling Library and realizing it looks exactly like a gothic cathedral. It's walking through Cross Campus and taking in a view that could easily go on a postcard and passing all the unique buildings on your way to section.

Yale is standing at the pinnacle of the arts. Yale is getting swept away in the moment as you're listening to the Yale Symphony Orchestra play at Woolsey Hall or immersed in the unbelievably incredible voices of the Glee Club or the renowned Whiffenpoofs. It's having your breath taken away by a student art exhibition or sitting in the Off Broadway Theater and being absolutely mesmerized by the YaleDancers performance.

Yale is diverse. Yale is your suitemates all having totally different backgrounds and beliefs and being able to talk to them about everything from culture to politics to your deepest philosophies and realizing they're entirely different from you but that's okay. It's every person being interested in something completely new and having the opportunity to learn about people's passions—whether you're having coffee at Blue State and discussing a friend's groundbreaking biomedical engineering work or 1 AM Facebook stalking and discovering the person you just met is the star of a major Broadway musical. It's realizing your differences are what make you unique and these differences are to be celebrated because you too are amazing.

Yale is intellectual. Yale is staying up until three in the morning contemplating the beginning of the universe with your best friend, and then going to Astronomy the next day and actually scientifically calculating the Big Bang with a world-renowned professor. Yale is debating politics with your roommate one moment and thinking up policies on how to reduce homelessness in New Haven in the next. It's taking a class with one professor and then learning about that same professor in the next class—immersing yourself in dozens of courses, from the study of the color blue to natural disasters to Aristotle's way of thinking, and falling in love with every one of them.

Yale is full of opportunity. Yale is having every possible course at your fingertips. It's hundreds of on-campus organizations that span every single interest you have and even all those you don't. It's knowing that every summer, every recess, every break, there are hundreds of study abroad programs, service trips, and more available to you. It's having the community of a residential college while still being immersed in the large campus life experience. It's learning to be part of not only the Yale community but the New Haven community—whether that's through political campaigns, community service, city organizations, or just getting to know the people you share the city with. It's access to internationally renowned professors through just an email or a walk down the street. It's a world of the most incredible reserve of books, and a community of upperclassman and faculty who are assigned to you by chance but become your family by choice.

Yale is learning that it's okay that you don't want to do pre-med anymore, or your passion is no longer poetry, or you can't handle a class, or you're interested in something else. It's discovering that yes, you do want to join that political campaign, or try out for that dance troupe, or volunteer in the Dominican Republic, learn Arabic, take a course about the origins of our universe, go to the best pizza restaurant in the U.S., cheer until your throat burns at games, open up to your freshman counseling group about your deepest fears, or get coffee with that one professor you can't help but admire.

Yale is discovering your passions. Yale is falling in love with a beautiful, awe-inspiring college and everyone in it. Yale is finding your family away from home.

THE ROAD TO YALE

Chapter

3

By the Numbers

THE ROAD TO YALE

CHAPTER THREE

Grades and Test Scores
Reported by authors

GRADES AND CLASS RANK

When admissions officers review applicant transcripts, they consider the rigor of the classes taken. In most schools, honors and AP/IB classes are weighted more than regular classes.

The GPAs for students in this book range from 3.80 to 4.00 (95 to 100) on unweighted GPA or 4.42 to 5.59 on weighted GPA. The class ranks for students in this book range from valedictorian to top 4% for large public schools and valedictorian to top 15% for small private and small public schools.

The number of AP classes/IB classes taken before senior year ranges from 3 to 12 per student. This number largely depends on how many such classes are available at each school. This group of students reported AP scores of 5s (63 scores), 4s (10), and 3s (5).

SAT AND ACT SCORES

Number of Students	SAT/ACT Score	SAT II Score	Number of SAT IIs per student
3	2400	800	3–5
4	2350–2399	750–800	2–5
5	2300–2349	730–800	2–3
2	2250–2299	750–800	2–3
1	32	—	—

THE ROAD TO YALE

Chapter

4

Alex

**PUBLIC HIGH SCHOOL
UNITED STATES**

Public High School, U.S.

Freshman	Sophomore	Junior	Senior
Gifted English	IB/AP Gifted English 1	IB/AP Gifted English 2	College English
Gifted AP World History	IB/AP Gifted History	IB/AP Gifted U.S. Government	College Economics
IB/AP Calculus SL	IB Math HL	IB Further Math	IB Further Math II
IB/AP Chemistry SL	IB/AP Biology SL	IB/AP Environment Science	College International Politics
Psychology	IB/AP Gifted Physics SL	IB/AP Gifted Physics HL	College Public Speaking
Spanish 3	IB Spanish 4 SL	IB/AP Spanish 5 HL	Computer Graphics
Web Publishing	Theory of Knowledge	Theory of Knowledge	GHSP Internship
9th Core PE	Health	Metal Design	GHSP Internship
	Sport for PE	CAS/Extended Essay	Racquet Sports

Alex

EXTRACURRICULARS AND WORK EXPERIENCE

City Youth Link Council, Vice president, Board of Directors youth liaison (6–12)
Chinese School, Math TA, substitute teacher (9–11)
Creative writing (8–12)
Future Problem Solving International Club, President (6–12)
Math Club, Club officer (3–12)
Science research, Research intern (10–12)
Sports teams, Member (9–12)
Youth Connection and Outspoken newspaper, Editor, journalist (6–12)

SUMMER ACTIVITIES

University of Washington, Research intern (12)
Stony Brook University, Garcia Center Summer Research Scholar (11)
Math camp, Teacher (11)
Local youth organization, Intern (10)
University of Washington, SIMUW Scholar (9)
University of Washington Robinson Center, Student (8)

AWARDS AND HONORS

Academics

National Merit Scholar (12)
AP Scholar with Distinction (11)
International Baccalaureate Diploma (11)
National AP Scholar (10)
Mathematical Association of America, American Invitational Mathematics Examination Qualifier (9–12)
State math competitions, Top 10 Individual, First Place Team (9–12)
International Future Problem Solving Competition, Top 10 Individual (9–11)
State Future Problem Solving Competition, First Place Individual (9–11)

Service

Youth Leadership Award, City and School District (12)
Most Valuable Player Youth Leadership Award (11)
Presidential Volunteer Service Award (11)

Arts

Scholastic Art & Writing Awards, Personal Essay & Memoir, Silver Key (10)
New Voices Awards, First Place, Excellent Award (8–9)

COMMON APPLICATION ESSAY

Recount an incident or time when you experienced failure. How did it affect you, and what lessons did you learn? (250-650 words)

The bathroom counter was covered with test tubes, a funnel, pipettes, growth medium, and a malodorous bottle of *Halobacterium salinarum*. The smell was not harmful, but it would have been great to have a gas mask. I carefully poured out 12 mL of growth medium into each of 25 test tubes and meticulously measured out 3 mL of *Halobacterium* for each one.

It was a stinky start to my independent research project in summer 2012. Fascinated by my AP Biology class, I looked into common experiment organisms. I studied one in particular, *H. salinarum*, learning about its photosynthetic properties and its excellence as a candidate for laboratory experiments. Expanding our knowledge of this life form could lead to a better understanding of photosynthesis, upon which human life depends. I decided to conduct a controlled experiment on *H. salinarum*'s growth patterns in varying light conditions to confirm its known behavior. The microbe's internal protein, called bacteriorhodopsin, is essential for its photosynthetic growth.

As I planned my project, I realized I did not have the equipment needed to measure amounts of bacteriorhodopsin. I needed help. After approaching several scientists in the field during the spring and summer, I finally obtained permission to conduct my protein analysis using a sophisticated instrument called a mass spectrophotometer, a machine that measures the absorption of light by various proteins, at the Seattle Institute for Systems Biology (ISB).

Access to this machine was provided on one condition—I had to culture my cells at home. Eagerly, I turned a closet into a darkroom, setting up some test tubes to bathe in the gentle glow of a 40W Sylvania incandescent bulb while others suffered in total darkness. For the next 40 days, my attention was on those little tubes. Every three days, I measured the growth of my *Halobacterium*. Despite my mom's reluctance, I preserved samples in my refrigerator and waited for the chance to go to the ISB labs. I fully expected the results of my intensive labors to be comparable to findings of similar investigations.

Nervousness consumed me as I walked into the ISB building on judgment day. I filled a well plate, placed it in the spectrophotometer, and waited anxiously as it ticked away dispassionately with my lab samples, taking measurements. When the graphs finally loaded, I was stunned. I couldn't believe that my samples had produced only one noticeable absorption peak between 400 and 700 nm wavelengths of light, instead of two. As I documented my work, I was disappointed and dissatisfied. What had caused my experiment to fail?

I reviewed my notes, consulted experts, and double-checked my methodology. My research revealed that the incandescent bulb I had used to grow *H. salinarum* did not emit a full spectrum of light and therefore caused my experiment to fall short of expectations.

Despite the undesirable results, I learned a great deal from this independent research project. Getting many no's from people in the early stages of the project was frustrating, but had I given up, I would have sunk the ship before it left port. I learned the virtue of persistence and patience through that process. Despite the smelly obstacles in conducting the experiment at home, I recognized that my desire to learn was stronger than any discomfort. I came to understand that even the smallest of details can be significant—a lesson that I intend never to forget in my future scientific and life endeavors.

Scientific research requires intelligence, creativity, hard work, critical thinking, and an open mind. The world around me is mysterious, exciting, and waiting for discovery. As I pursue future scientific inquiry, I can expect many more failures and successes, but I will always be learning. I will continue exploring and cannot wait—someday my unexpected results may lead to an exciting breakthrough.

SUPPLEMENTAL ESSAY

In this essay, please reflect on something you would like us to know about you that we might not learn from the rest of your application, or on something about which you would like to say more. You may write about anything—from personal experiences or interests to intellectual pursuits. (500 words or less)

Seattle is often associated with individual and corporate wealth. Companies like Microsoft, Amazon, and Starbucks provide comfortable jobs, yet 15% of the population still struggles to get by below the poverty line. Growing up in a relatively well-off suburban neighborhood made it hard to appreciate the social and economic diversity of my community.

Starting in sixth grade, my involvement with a youth service organization called Youth Link has brought me face-to-face with disadvantaged members of my city. Every year, we collect and distribute outerwear as part of an event called the Kid's Care Coat Drive. Through this event, we help clothe hundreds of families and protect them from the cold Seattle winters. One year, while surrounded by piles of coats, I found myself guiding a family in Spanish as they searched for warm jackets to wear. The teenage son needed a hooded jacket to cover his threadbare shirt. As I rummaged through the remaining piles of clothes, I found a familiar hooded coat—I had donated it myself earlier. I handed over the coat to the teen. He slipped it on slowly, looked at his mother, and beamed with appreciation. I was happy that I did what I could to help, but it bothered me to know I had spare jackets to donate, yet he had none of his own to wear. I wished that I could do more.

As I grew older, my desire to help others inspired me to take on more responsibilities in Youth Link. I have helped organize Thanksgiving dinners, food donations, and coat drives to benefit the needy. Last year, we collected over 1,500 coats for hundreds of needy families. I am humbled by the determination of the impoverished families we assist. They are living proof that my charitable service can make a difference in other people's lives.

Making a difference in my community has been rewarding. My involvement has nurtured my growth from a shy volunteer to an outspoken leader. Though I still sort clothes, I have improved my public speaking skills through presentations to the Youth Link council and the city council, and my time management skills through organizing meetings and events. Youth Link has provided me with a wholesome context for developing as a person and citizen, and to practice the values of learning, charity, and care. I want to continue to use my talents to aid those around me and make a positive impact in my community.

WHY YALE

What in particular about Yale has influenced your decision to apply?
(100 words or less)

Yale is a great liberal arts school and I intend to pursue a liberal arts education because I believe a broad understanding of the world is necessary to solve global issues. I am specifically interested in environmental challenges like clean energy and water quality, and Yale's Environmental Engineering Program and Center for Green Chemistry and Green Engineering are an excellent fit for my interests and aspirations. I was also extremely impressed by the intellectual atmosphere during my visit last summer. The enthusiasm and breadth of knowledge displayed by the students I met were inspiring and mirrors my approach to education.

ADDITIONAL QUESTIONS

You have been granted a free weekend next month. How will you spend it?
I will write a short story. I enjoy writing science fiction about futuristic dystopias.

What is something about which you have changed your mind in the last three years?
I used to find economics uninteresting but a lecture on patents convinced me that incentives directly impact scientific advancements.

What is the best piece of advice you have received while in high school?
"Love the things you do." — This advice from my best friend inspired me to devote more energy to community service work.

What do you wish you were better at being or doing?
Self-reflection. My desire for self-improvement is an important aspect of my character, yet I find it difficult to ask myself the right questions.

What is a learning experience, in or out of the classroom that has had a significant impact on you?
My Future Problem Solving experience taught me that scientific advances must be coupled with economic and political awareness for the greatest impact.

THE ROAD TO YALE

Chapter

5

Charlie

PRIVATE HIGH SCHOOL
PEOPLE'S REPUBLIC OF CHINA

Private High School, China

Freshman	Sophomore	Junior	Senior
English 9	English 10	AP English Literature	AP English Language
Algebra II	Advanced Pre-Calculus	AP Calculus BC	AP European History
General Biology	Intro Chemistry (one semester)	General Chemistry	AP Biology
World Geography (one semester)	Intro Physics (one semester)	AP U.S. History	AP Psychology
Spanish II	Modern World History	IB Spanish B SL	IB Spanish B SL
Health/Drivers Ed (one semester)	Chinese VI	IB Chinese B HL	IB Chinese B HL
Cross Country	PHE (physical and health education)	Stagecraft (one semester)	Stagecraft (one semester)
	Photography		

Before High School and Outside Classes
Algebra
Geometry
Spanish I

Charlie

EXTRACURRICULARS AND WORK EXPERIENCE

Confection: Literary Magazine, Editor-in-Chief (10–12)
National English Honor Society (11–12)
National Honor Society (11–12)
Varsity Cross Country (9–12)
Varsity Dance (10–12)
Varsity Forensics (11)
Varsity Track and Field (9–12)
Writing (5–12)

SUMMER ACTIVITIES

Kenyon Young Writer's Workshop, Alpha SF/F/H Workshop for Young Writers (12)
University of Virginia, Young Writer's Workshop (11)
Cal National Debate Institute (11)
California State Summer School of Arts (10)

AWARDS AND HONORS

Academics

National Merit Scholar (12)
Wellesley Book Award (11)

Arts

National Young Arts Foundation, Merit Award (12)
Scholastic Art & Writing Awards, National Gold Medals, National Silver Medals
(Senior Portfolio), Regional Gold and Silver Keys (7–12)

COMMON APPLICATION ESSAY

Some students have a background or story so central to their identity that they believe their application would be incomplete without it. Share this story. (250–650 words)

SHANGHAI

I have a curious choice to make every time I pronounce this city's name, like deciding between two sides of a conflict: do I speak in the tongue of the town I was born in or in the language of the land I live in?

"SHANG-hai." I come as a foreigner, accenting the first syllable, twisting the 'A' into the curve of my lips as the word twangs in my mouth. Born and bred in Californian sunshine, I hated this city of haze at first with a simmering fire in my gut that clawed its way into notebooks full of acrid words. A prisoner of my father's job, I discovered in the next six months that no amount of steamed buns could fill that hole in my soul where my hometown used to be. I burned my first bridges in that flight across the Pacific; left drifting, I struggled to learn how to pronounce the slang of the city like a local, to acclimatize my tongue to the new way names rolled from my lips.

"ShangHA-AI." But sometimes I defend the besieged stronghold, my adopted city, opening up the soft palate so 'ah' comes out in the first syllable before bouncing through the second one. Accents make all the difference in local supermarkets here, where the slightest slip-up in your vowels can expose you as nonnative. But now, that fear doesn't stop me from chatting with taxi drivers on my way to dance practice anymore; every person I can convince that I'm not foreign-born is a small victory in the uphill battle of learning the language of my parents.

Adjusting to life in China requires more than a tectonic shift of mindset; reality lies in a long war of attrition—a personal ten-year siege of Troy. I did not embrace Shanghai all at once; slowly, haltingly, I accepted truces. Late night strolls weren't so bad, I admitted, and the new people—friends from Canada, Denmark, New Jersey, and even the sandwich deli lady—were as fascinating and compelling as any Greek or Trojan hero. Through conversations as short as ordering a vegetarian panini or as long as shared plane flights to a forensics competition, they helped me realize that unhappiness has always been a choice. I needed to reassess the values that directed my life, to look around with wonder instead of prejudice. Because even after the war ended and Troy fell, it was rebuilt; and even as I fought air pollution and reckless drivers, idiomatic grammar and my own biases, Shanghai reforged me with the defiance of its people and the steel of its skyscrapers. Wars don't make people; wars change people.

Two years later, I smile at the shopkeepers I once feared, switching languages as easily as jackets. I make small talk with security guards and savor the rare days of pollution-free air. Now I see the fortune I have to live in an international forum, filled with snapshots of lives across cultures and continents—a place where we can learn from each other even as we laugh, where we sing the cadences of our sentences that pay homage to our countries of origin.

"I live in—Shanghai." I still wobble between accents, stumbling before the word as I remember where I am. "But I'm originally from California." Sometimes, my American tongue wins out; others, Chinese rolls from my lips with rich authenticity. Language used to mark the front where my cultures clashed with each other. Now, it opens new paths that lead me off into undiscovered regions, familiar and exotic. This internal war has given me open palms and words in three languages, grounded me in knowing who I am and what I love, and made me ready to adapt to and appreciate the world, wherever the winds blow me.

SUPPLEMENTAL ESSAY

Please reflect on something you would like us to know about you that we might not learn from the rest of your application, or on something you would like to say more. You may write about anything—from personal experiences or interests to intellectual pursuits. (500 words or less)

Would you look at that, I thought, staring down at the paper. *Plan B actually worked.*

I held the very first copy of *Confection: A Literary Magazine* in my hands, its black-and-white pages still warm from the printer. Handling each sheet gingerly, I scanned the familiar spreads. There was Aaron, grinning cheekily from his double page. Below, Tiffany's artwork spidered across the margins in graceful lines. I knew each photo, each page, each pica. I had fought with the formatting and font sizes and laid out all the columns and captions, stealing minutes between classes and hours from my sleep to tweak the designs and rearrange the poems yet again. Thirty-two pages slowly emerged from the art and writing that my fellow high schoolers had submitted.

"You can keep the advance copy," the lady who ran the print center said kindly, and I stammered out a thanks.

Here is a confession: I'd never run a magazine before.

Here is another confession: I made it up as I went along.

When the original editor-in-chief unexpectedly abdicated, the literary magazine club fell into my inexperienced hands. I was just beginning my second year at a new school overseas and trying to handle a club that had held only two meetings last year — once to meet each other, and once for the yearbook photo.

That wouldn't cut it this year, I decided. Writing outside of class wasn't especially popular among kids who often spoke a different language at home. I wanted to give them the opportunity to see their work in print to spur their continued interest.

There was a slight problem in this otherwise bulletproof plan: no one else in the club knew the mechanics of making a magazine, and not many had the time to learn how to wrangle the layout software into obedience. During first semester, publication stalled as I tried to teach club members about pica blocks while coaxing them to write in their free time.

Once second semester hit the ground, however, the deadline for getting printed loomed ominously close. There simply wasn't enough *time* for everyone to reach the fluency in InDesign needed to lay out their own pages before exam season.

Thus, plan B came into play — with a single-minded intensity and my typical bulldog tenacity, I threw myself into laying out the entire magazine on my own. Club members contributed with material; I wrestled the poems into place, matchmade artwork with fiction, and even found a company willing to defray the printing costs in exchange for advertising. In less than a month, the pages grew into the literary magazine that I now held in my hands.

As I headed towards the high school, a slow grin overtook my face. This was a publication made by high schoolers, and high schoolers alone — not a single teacher had a hand in it.

Aaron waved to me from the bleachers. I waved back, holding up the copy of *Confection*. "Litmag's out," I called triumphantly.

WHY YALE?

What in particular about Yale has influenced your decision to apply?
(100 words or less)

After my journeys across continents and adventures in three languages, I've discovered that literature forms rare stability in my existence of flux. I hope to meet fellow travelers at Yale University, which recognizes the global nature of great works in its literature major by requiring students to supplement their learning with a foreign language, allowing them to broaden their understanding of how literature shapes human ideas. With varied areas of study and the seminar-style core classes that allow for in-depth pursuit of the material, the literature major at Yale embodies the unique, comprehensive, and versatile literary experience I desire.

ADDITIONAL QUESTIONS

What excites you intellectually, really?
Understanding how everything fits into the bigger picture. Studying the epilogue of McCarthy's *Blood Meridian* to understand the book, the converging events of European history, and the role of oxygen in aging all share the same moment of oh wow.

Think about a disappointment you have experienced. What was your response?
Once, I came out of a dance exchange feeling like I'd wasted a day. I asked myself 'why' several times before finally discovering that I'd foolishly been clinging onto something called dignity. I made sure to leave that at the door the next time.

Suite-style living may be an integral part of your Yale College experience. What would you contribute to the dynamic of your suite?
Strategic Douglas Adams quotes to lighten the mood. At least three languages. Fountain pens. A ready ear and a readier hug. Poetry. Extra everything — clothes, Ace bandages, bad jokes. A dog-like love of Frisbee. Inspirational Tolkien upon demand.

What do you wish you were better at being or doing?
Saying the obvious. Often underrated, I've discovered that it becomes a good strategy in defusing arguments and awkward situations, refocusing philosophy debates, defining the parameters of an experiment, and clarifying difficult problems.

THE ROAD TO YALE

Chapter

6

Emma

PUBLIC HIGH SCHOOL
UNITED STATES

Public High School, U.S.

Freshman	Sophomore	Junior	Senior
Honors English I	Honors English II	AP English Language	AP English Literature
Honors Algebra II	Honors Pre-Calculus	AP Calculus BC	AP Statistics
Honors Biology	AP Biology	AP Chemistry	AP Physics C
Honors World Geography	AP World History	AP U.S. History	AP U.S. Government and AP Macroeconomics
Honors Spanish II	Honors Spanish III	AP Spanish IV	AP Spanish Literature V
Technology	Honors Chemistry	AP Computer Science	Online Multivariable
Tennis	Honor and AP Psychology	Honors Physics	Teacher's assistant

Before High School and Outside Classes

Honors Algebra I	Speech & Communications
Geometry (CBE)	Honors Spanish I
Art (online and CBE)	Health (online)

Emma

EXTRACURRICULARS AND WORK EXPERIENCE

Community service non-profit, Co-founder (7–12)
Creative Writing, National and local online newspaper blogger (5–12)
Habitat for Humanity Club, President and co-founder (9–12)
Debate Team, Vice president (9–12)
National Spanish Honor Society, Vice president (10–12)
Tennis (8–10)
Physics/Robotics Club, Vice president (9–12)
Ping pong (7–12)

SUMMER ACTIVITIES

Stony Brook University, Simons Summer Research Fellow (11)
Texas Children's Hospital, Research intern (10)
Chinese-American Outstanding Youth Cultural Camp, China (9)

AWARDS AND HONORS

Academics

National Merit Scholar (12)
Biology Olympiad, Semifinalist (11)
Lincoln–Douglas Debate, UIL Invitational Meet, Second Place (11)
Lincoln–Douglas Debate, UIL Districts, First Place (10)
Debate Team Sweepstakes, UIL Invitational Meet, First Place (10)
Future Problem Solving Program International, FPS Scenario Writing, State Finalist (9–11)

Service

PARADE Magazine, All-American High School Service Team Award (11)
Youth Service America, Harris Wofford Youth Award (10)
Build-A-Bear Workshop, Huggable Heroes National Finalist (9)

Arts

Scholastic Art & Writing Awards, Science Fiction, National Gold Medal (10–11)
Scholastic Art & Writing Awards, Science Fiction, Personal Essays, Poetry, Region-at-Large Gold Keys (9–12)

Athletics

Ping Pong tournaments, area tournaments, First to Fourth Places (9–12)
Congressional Award, Silver and Gold Medals (10–11)

COMMON APPLICATION ESSAY
Some students have a background or story so central to their identity that they believe their application would be incomplete without it. Share this story. (250–650 words)

Silver Change

The sky was an exhilarating blue, and the sun blazed on my sweat-drenched back. Taking a deep breath, I lifted my hand to the door and knocked. After a few seconds, the door cracked open just enough for someone's clear blue eye to peek through, and I began to speak before I could get cut off with the "no, we're not interested, thank you" that I had heard so many times before.

"Hello, my name is Emma, and I'm raising money for the earthquake victims in China. Would you like to make a donation?" I held out the handmade donation box I had made the night before from an old shoebox. *Please help*, it read, *because so many people are dead*.

At 12 years old, I got my first taste of death on a wide-screen TV. Images of collapsed buildings and misshapen bodies had seared themselves into my mind with a burn that made it impossible not to do something. To my surprise, however, not many volunteer organizations were willing to employ twelve year olds—so I had taken things into my own hands. Here I was, a pre-teen in ratty sneakers and a too-big T-shirt, with an almost-empty box of cash clutched in one hand and a homemade newsletter in the other, going door-to-door in a town where the word Sichuan meant little more than the quaint Chinese restaurant down the road.

A young boy was standing in the doorway, and for the first time, I saw someone whose eyes mirrored the sadness in mine. Of all the adults I had talked to that afternoon, not one of them seemed to grasp the sheer, cripplingly devastation I felt. Adults have had their own brushes with death—I had not. "My parents aren't home right now," he began. I was about to turn around when he opened his clenched fist, where a handful of silver change glimmered in his outstretched palm. He handed it to me, and added apologetically, "Sorry I don't have any mor—Wait!" He dug his hands deep into his pockets, searching, and finally came out with two nickels, a dime, and three old pennies. He handed the coins to me as well, and gave me another hopeful smile. "I hope this helps."

In that moment, my smile mirrored his as well.

It's been over four years since May 12, 2008. I'm older now, and maybe wiser—I'd like to think so. More importantly, I've started what I promised the twelve year-old me that I would do: change the world. The money I raised that day has multiplied exponentially. The newsletter I made has become ten, twenty, thirty. My one-person quest to make a difference has grown from a backyard effort to a non-profit my two siblings and I founded. Our organization has raised more than $40,000 for over 14,000 disaster victims in not just China, but Haiti, Japan, and the U.S.

There is still nothing worth more to me than those few, precious seconds when a boy with golden hair and glittering eyes the same color as the skies above emptied his pockets for a cause he had never even heard of. I hope he knows that there are 14,000 people out there who would like to thank him...and that I am one of them.

SUPPLEMENTAL ESSAY

In this essay, please reflect on something you would like us to know about you that we might not learn from the rest of your application, or on something about which you would like to say more. You may write about anything—from personal experiences or interests to intellectual pursuits. (500 words or less)

Purple Gloves

The Department of Health claims that the most common way to contract the black plague (*Yersinia pestis*) is through flea or rat bites. I politely disagree. The most common way is to spend seven weeks in a white lab coat and purple nitrile gloves. Over the course of two summers, I've gone through over seventy pairs of purple nitrile gloves...none of which have fit me properly. However, Kimberly-Clark doesn't manufacture "just right" as a glove size; if they do, my lab was always understandably out of stock.

I pulled out two crinkled gloves from the box emblazoned with the black letters XS and valiantly attempted to squeeze my fingers into the too-small gloves. No luck. I moved to the next box, one with the letter S marked on the side in crisp black ink. Too big. I had an uncomfortable recollection of the same situation occurring to Goldilocks, only she at least had a size that was "just right." But I was a thousand miles from home and there didn't seem to be anything "just right" in this sterile environment, where my gloves were too big and my lab coat seemed to wrinkle no matter how I folded it each afternoon before I left.

There were days when nothing seemed "just right", like the day I arrived at lab at 7:00 a.m. to start my experiment, and the entire building was pitch-black, but I groped around until I found the light switch and set up my materials within an hour...only to find out that the enzyme I needed hadn't arrived yet. I spent the next nine hours reading papers on *Yersinia pestis*. Or my very first day at lab, when my hand shook so much I spilled the plague all over my lab station. If anyone asks, though, I'll blame it on the too-big gloves.

But there were also days when my gloves didn't seem that big, days when everything seemed to fall into place. There were days when all my DNA bands showed up, days when I caught a mistake before it happened. There were days when I had just enough bacteria for all my microtubes, days when I had hundreds of colonies on my agar plate and for once, I could choose which colony of bacteria I wanted to use for my experiment instead of poking in a pipet tip blindly and hoping that what I was getting was bacteria and not agar. Those days, I'd leave the lab with feeling the same way I did on my very first day in a lab coat: young and naïve, yes, but also endlessly hopeful about the possibilities of the future.

Because I don't want a nine-to-five job. I want an eight-to-five job, a nine-to-six job. I want a job that starts before the sun breaks past the horizon and a job that ends when the sun's rays have already bid their farewells to the velvet sky. I want a job that exhausts me, a job that challenges me, a job...like research. I want a job with purple gloves and a white lab coat and experiments that are never "just right" but always my best effort, because research may be exhausting, but there's something exhilarating in working on the cutting-edge of a field, being one of many that are striving to mold a better future for us and for our children, and although not all research experiments are successful, my research experience—from reading papers to wearing purple nitrile gloves to presenting my project at the end-of-the-program symposium—has always been.

WHY YALE

What in particular about Yale has influenced your decision to apply?
(100 words or less)

Falling in Love

I'm 17 and I've fallen in love with books, with science, with service... and with Yale, because in Yale I found a school that was vast in its offerings yet seemed tailored specifically to me. I can't help but want to get involved in everything, from continuing my debate experience with Urban Debate League to combining my 5 years of Spanish with my love of service in MAS Familias. I know that at Yale, I will fall in love all over again, not just with the campus but with everything that it offers.

ADDITIONAL QUESTIONS

What would you do with a free afternoon tomorrow?
I would sit by the park and re-read Calvin & Hobbes.

What is the best piece of advice you have received in the last three years?
You will never get back this moment.

If you could witness one moment in history, what would it be and why?
The completion of the Human Genome Project, for the promises it holds.

What do you wish you were better at being or doing?
I wish I were less impatient.

What is something about which you have changed your mind in the last three years?
Falafel, which I once disliked. Also, genetic engineering — we will one day have the ability, and the obligation, to shape our future.

THE ROAD TO YALE

Chapter

7

Eric

PUBLIC HIGH SCHOOL
UNITED STATES

Public High School, U.S. (9–10)
State Academy of Math and Science (11–12)

Freshman	Sophomore	Junior	Senior
Honors English I	Honors English II	Honors Prin Biology I, II	Mechanics, Electr and Magnetism
Honors Geometry	Honors Algebra II	Honors Prin Biology Lab I, II	Mechanics, Electr and Magnetism Lab
Honors Biology	Honors Chemistry	Honors Gen Chem I, II	Organic Chemistry I, II
Honors Humanities	AP World History	Honors Gen Chem Lab I, II	U.S. from 1865, U.S. to 1865
Honors Spanish II	Honors Chinese III	Writing About Lit I, II	World Literature I, II
Honors Chinese II	AP European History	Pre-Calculus	Calculus II, Applied Statistics
AP Human Geography	Honors Orchestra	Calculus I	VOICE, Entrepreneurship
Orchestra		American Government	

Before High School and Outside Classes
Honors Algebra I

Spanish I

Chinese I (CBE)

Eric

EXTRACURRICULARS AND WORK EXPERIENCE

Aspire for Research Organization, Director (11–12)
Camp Summit (11)
Community Youth Leadership Camp, Assistant counselor (9–11)
Dallas Youth Volunteer Association, Co-chair (11–12)
IndePedals (Science technology company), Co-founder (11–12)
Forward Tutoring, Outreach director (11–12)
High school LASER Club, President (10)
Nursing home, Volunteer (9–12)
High school full orchestra, Concertmaster (10)
Science research (9–12)
Swimming, Coach (1–9)

SUMMER ACTIVITIES

Community Youth Leadership Camp (9–12)
University of Texas at Dallas, Nanoexplorers Program, Lab intern (9–12)

AWARDS AND HONORS

Academics
National Merit Scholar (12)
Siemens Westinghouse, Regional Semifinalist (12)
University of North Texas President's Research Award (12)
Siemens Westinghouse Regional Competition, Finalist (11)
State Chemistry Science Olympiad, First Place (11)
State Protein Modeling Science Olympiad, Second Place (11)
Chinese Institute of Engineering Young Achiever's Award (10)
Texas Junior Academy of Science, Second Place (10)
Texas Junior Science and Humanities Symposium, Semifinalist (10)
International Chinese Essay Writing Contest, First Place (9)
Exxon Mobil Texas State Science and Engineering Fair, Fourth Place (11–12)
Regional Science and Engineering Fair, Second Place (11–12)
University of North Texas President's List (11–12)

Performing Arts
Exemplary Soloist Award/Superior Solo/ Ensemble (9–10)
All-Region and All-Area Orchestra (9–11)

Business
New Venture Creation Contest, Finalist (12)
Princeton Business Plan Competition, Semifinalist (11)
Dell Social Innovation Challenge, First Place (12)
Texas Economics Challenge, Finalist and Top Score (11)

COMMON APPLICATION ESSAY

Evaluate a significant experience, achievement, risk you have taken, or ethical dilemma you have faced and its impact on you. (250-650 words)

Aspire

I stared aimlessly at the wall, frustrated by the dilemma I was in. As an executive of my school's Research Organization, I was expected to fulfill my duties before each club meeting. In just twelve hours, we were about to unveil our new non-profit competition, which was unique in its concept of providing scholarships to underprivileged students without research opportunities. As the originator and director of this initiative, I had the responsibility of giving the competition a name.

Easy enough, right? The task should have taken me no longer than ten minutes, but the ideas that came to mind weren't what I expected. I needed something more creative, a name that would capture the true meaning of what the competition was designed to do.

Later that day, I came upon a news article with "Inspiring girl wins big at national science competition!" in bold print as the headline news for the day. The story was about a girl named Samantha Garvey who was named an Intel STS semifinalist for her research work. Reading what seemed to be a typical research story, I soon discovered that Samantha was actually homeless. As a student who lived in a homeless shelter, Samantha found work at a local research laboratory to bolster her family's economic situation. Motivated to fulfill the dreams of her family, Samantha was determined to seize her opportunity and impact the lives of those around her.

When I saw this girl's story, I was reminded of my own journey as a young scientist. Although I may not have been homeless, I can connect with the passion Samantha had for research. It's a passion that transcends the spoils of winning a national competition or simply the pride that comes with making a research discovery; it's about supporting those you love and helping to shape others' futures, a value that is commonly lost amidst the competitive nature of teenage life. All great scientists start as ordinary science enthusiasts, born with a curiosity and aspiration to make a change in this world. Fortunate enough to be able to pursue my own research aspirations; I believe that there are millions of people just like Samantha in this world, ordinary people who just needed that opportunity, that catalyst, to reach their own aspirations, too.

Before the meeting began, I felt a spark beginning to brighten the once dull light bulb that sat above my head. Samantha's story exemplifies what the American Dream is all about: when given an opportunity coupled with a strong passion, anything can be accomplished. When I think of Samantha Garvey, I think of the students who will be affected by this competition, how these students are the future of our world, and how their dreams can come to fruition by my efforts. I knew the exact name I wanted to give my competition.

When it was time to reveal the name, I proudly stood at the podium, and without a doubt of my decision, I announced:

"Introducing the *Aspire* science competition!"

SUPPLEMENTAL ESSAY

In this essay, please reflect on something you would like us to know about you that we might not learn from the rest of your application, or on something about which you would like to say more. You may write about anything—from personal experiences or interests to intellectual pursuits. (500 words or less)

On my sixteenth birthday, my father gave me an old and tattered notebook. With its rotting pages starting to crumble and layers of dust marring its faded text, the notebook shattered my hopes for a gift worthy of a sixteenth birthday. As if my father could sense my disappointment, he told me in a very serious tone: "Discover the value of this book as it documents three generations of our family's legacy." Curious as to how such an antiquated object could be so important to my father, I decided to read the book and find out for myself.

Early-20th century: My great-grandfather was a local doctor for a small Chinese village during the Qing Dynasty. Despite his valued expertise, he accepted little to no pay from his patients. When my grandfather asked why he rarely accepted payment, he answered, "Money does not satisfy the heart; only the warmth of love makes life worth living." As he preached the importance of selflessness, this was the last line he wrote in his notebook.

Mid-20th century: World War II was at its peak of conflict when a Japanese aircraft had bombed the village where my grandfather lived. Fortunate enough to survive the attack, my grandfather foraged through the ruins of his house and saved the notebook. When he escaped to Nanjing, he witnessed the suffering of both the wounded and traumatized soldiers. Inspired by my great-grandfather's efforts as well as those of the sacrificing soldiers, my grandfather enrolled as a volunteer medic. By the time the war ended, my grandfather retired from his temporary medical work, but he continued to express the undying inspiration he felt to help others in his notebook.

Late-20th century: During the Cultural Revolution in China, the government assigned my father to do labor in the countryside. While accomplishing his tasks, my father also found interest in the rural herbs. He studied the herbs, identified the ones with medicinal value, and administered medicine to the other workers. It was from this job that he expressed an intellectual passion in the notebook that my grandfather and great-grandfather once possessed, as numerous drawings of herbs were recorded followed by the names of those who needed that particular medicine.

Now as the owner of the notebook that carries the legacy of my heritage, I feel an overwhelming sense of honor. But more importantly, reading the notebook has made me recognize a responsibility. When I read the long list of names of the people my relatives helped treat, I feel inspired to make a similar impact on society. When I read about the century-long hardships my relatives had to overcome, I feel compelled to persevere through my own. As I pioneer the fields of cancer research today and aspire to do the same in the future, I will always carry this notebook. It reminds me of the love, inspiration, and intellectual passion that comes with helping others, and I strive to make my own mark on the proud legacy of my heritage.

WHY YALE?
What in particular about Yale has influenced your decision to apply? (100 words or less)

Beyond Yale's renowned prestige, entrepreneur Lei Zhang described Yale best when he donated $8,888,888 to Yale. He explained how Yale not only gave him the tools for financial management, but also instilled in him the necessity to give back. This educational philosophy has not only served him well but is the driver behind so many successful Yale alumni who want to serve their community. Inspired by his story, I hope to join the Yale family to personally experience this educational philosophy.

ADDITIONAL QUESTIONS
What would you do with a free afternoon tomorrow?
Play a game of pick-up basketball with old friends.

What is the best piece of advice you have received in the last three years?
"There are no shortcuts to success" —Dr. Richard Sinclair, Dean of TAMS, in his opening speech to the senior class.

If you could witness one moment in history, what would it be and why?
If I could witness the origin of the universe, I could answer both scientific and philosophical questions that have long been at the heart of the most controversial debates.

What do you wish you were better at being or doing?
From rocking out in the shower to obsessing over YouTube vocal sensation Sam Tsui, I wish I could sing like the rock star I have always imagined myself to be.

What is something about which you have changed your mind in the last three years?
Postponing my trip to Kenya last summer, I wish I could have made the trip with my new product Indepedals, which generates portable electricity to help third-world citizens.

THE ROAD TO YALE

Chapter

8

Jared

**PUBLIC HIGH SCHOOL
UNITED STATES**

Public High School, U.S.

Freshman	Sophomore	Junior	Senior
Honors English I	Honors English II	AP English Language and Composition	AP English Language and Composition
Honors Western Civilizations	AP U.S. History	Honors Government and Economics	Global Awareness
Honors Biology	Honors Chemistry	College Physics (U. of Maine)	AP Biology
Honors Geometry	Honors Algebra 2	Honors Pre-Calculus	College Calculus I (U. of Maine)
Health/Physical Education	AP Psychology	Theater	Technology Internship with school technology coordinator
Music Appreciation	Theater	French III	Theater
French I	French II		French IV
Band			

Before High School and Outside Classes

World Civilizations (Univ. of Maine at Fort Kent)

AP Computer Science (online)

AP Music Theory (online)

Jared

ACTIVITIES AND WORK EXPERIENCE

Aroostook Teen Leadership Camp, Camp staff and advisory board member, Weekend team student supervisor (9–12)

Catholic youth ministry, Planning board (8–12)

Church cantor (9–12)

Cross country, Co-captain (8–12)

Cross country skiing (6–12)

French club/exchange (10–12)

Key Club, President (9–12)

High school drama club, State All Festival Cast, Lead character (9–12)

National Honor Society, President (10–12)

Private music lessons (12)

Students Against Drunk Driving, President (9–12)

Student Council, Vice president, senior class representative (9–12)

Youth Voices (Substance abuse prevention group), Statewide awards (7–12)

SUMMER ACTIVITIES

Aroostook Teen Leadership Camp, Volunteer (9–12)

La Festival Jeunesse de L'Acadie, Maine representative (11)

AWARDS AND HONORS

Academics

AP Scholar with Honors (11)

Dartmouth Book Award (11)

French speech competition, Second Place (11)

Highest Achievement Awards, AP English, AP Psych, College Physics, AP U.S. History (9–11)

Rensselaer Medal Award (11)

Service

Humanitarian Heart Honorable Mention and Project Leader scholarships (10)

Performing Arts

All National Honor Ensembles' Mixed Choir (12)

All State Chorus (11, 12)

All Festival Cast, Regional and States (9–11)

Athletics

Cross Country Running, Most Improved Award (9), Varsity letter (10), All-Aroostook Award & State Qualifier (11–12)

Cross-country Skiing, Varsity letter (9), Most Improved Award (11), All-Aroostook Award & State qualifier (10–11), and Overall State Champions (10–12)

Dewey Dewitt Award (Scholar-Athlete Award) (9–12)

Track and Field, Varsity Letter (9) and All-Aroostook Award (11)

COMMON APPLICATION ESSAY

Describe a place or environment where you are perfectly content. What do you do or experience there, and why is it meaningful to you? (250-650 words)

During my junior year of high school, I moved homes and got my own bathroom. For a sixteen-year-old, this is second best to getting your own car. I was elated. I would no longer have to worry about my brothers taking candid photos of me on the toilet and sending them to family and friends. Those days were gone! I soon discovered, though, that the bathroom was a special place for me.

No, I didn't turn my bathroom into a bachelor pad or a man cave. I instead developed a liking for my bathroom because of its ulterior meaning to me. The bathroom became a place for me to unwind, to have Jared time. It's where I can process my day, Skype a long-distance friend, or just clear my mind. With my far from enjoyable digestive issues, my fondness of the bathroom is certainly questionable. Nevertheless, the bathroom provides me with time to myself. After a busy day of school, meetings, sports, play rehearsal, voice lessons, and homework, I go to the bathroom and I take some time to just slow down.

My bathroom does not have any windows. While some may view this as a ventilation concern, it actually makes my escape much more vivid. I live in a small rural community where a boy becomes a man when he buys a snowmobile; where hunting, fishing, and mudding are practically the high school sports; and where school closes for two weeks for potato harvest. And though I am not a vice-presidential candidate, it's also vital to mention that I can see Canada from my house. This town's rich French culture and close-knit community has truly benefited my upbringing and impacted my character. Though I'm grateful to have grown up here, the community has limited me in many ways. With passions such as the arts, education, and volunteerism, I tend to stick out like a sore thumb. Going to the bathroom and not having windows to see where I really am helps me imagine where and what I could be. With so many of my peers not planning on going to college, not leaving this area, and not pursuing their true passions, I occasionally fear that my dreams will become only a fantasy instead of an attainable objective. But with a map of our world hanging proudly on the wall, my windowless bathroom stimulates my inner dreamer. Though at times I may feel trapped, small, or limited, my bathroom supports me and all that I can become.

I play a lot of music in the bathroom. From classical to Indie rock, you're bound to find me singing something. Furthermore, while brushing my teeth I'll do a plie and practice my ballet positions. Yes, I like to dance. In fact, I've been dancing for years. Except being the only boy in dance class in this small town has been quite difficult. I was constantly teased and tormented. My bathroom is like my safe haven. I can sing and dance and no one will laugh. It's true: my bathroom allows me to freely express myself.

Some of my best work hails from my bathroom. I've watched TED talks and have felt inspired to make change. I've sent emails and organized service projects. I've practiced a French speech in front of my mirror and I've rehearsed audition songs as if I'm in a recording studio. The person I am today and my list of accomplishments would be very different if it were not for my discovery of the bathroom. Though I've been using one for nearly my whole life, I never realized the importance of my time spent in the bathroom. Without time to unwind, to think, and to discover myself, I wouldn't have the confidence to be the person I know I am. I am Jared and I respectfully submit this essay from my bathroom.

SUPPLEMENTAL ESSAY

In this essay, please reflect on something you would like us to know about you that we might not learn from the rest of your application, or on something about which you would like to say more. You may write about anything—from personal experiences or interests to intellectual pursuits. (500 words or less)

My stomach growled as I unwrapped yet another Pepto-bismol tablet. A quick glance in the box revealed only a few tablets remaining; I had ingested nearly half the box. I sat in an auditorium full of people as a bead of sweat trickled down my forehead. It was my first ever one act drama competition and I was feeling very sick. Yet to find the source of my maladies, I figured I had a stomach bug or perhaps even food poisoning.

A few peers suggested that I was merely nervous. I certainly had reason to be; as a freshman, lacking confidence and experience, I was to perform the lead role of our play in front of a large and distinguished audience. I shrugged this diagnosis away as I had never experienced similar symptoms from nervousness. After the forty-minute performance was over, I totally forgot about feeling queasy. I was feeling almost completely opposite actually; I experienced a sort of natural high. This led me to realize that I've never experienced such intense nervousness and trepidation because I've never cared so much about something. This seemingly silly moment in my high school career has left a large impact on the person I am and the person I want to become.

As I child I often entertained: I would dance for my family, sporting my silver sequenced cummerbund; I wrote and starred in my very own short plays, which often guest starred my mother; and I made relatives form a circle around me as I told a fanciful tale. Performing has always been something I've enjoyed doing - nothing more - until, what I like to call, my Pepto moment.

This Pepto moment made me realize that this is what I was meant to do. I've had other Pepto moments — moments when I've known that I'm in my element. Whether it be an academic competition, a leadership conference or a service trip to Guatemala, there have been times when I've felt like the truest version of myself. I loved what I was doing and I was good at it too — I was in my element.

After I discovered this passion, I began to pursue the performing arts much more. I sang in my church more frequently, I started taking voice lessons, and I read books upon books about different acting techniques. I even started taking dance class again, no longer worrying about the teasing I would have to endure. I also no longer worried that I was "wasting my academic talents" because I knew that was really only broadening my mind and that I would always be a lifelong learner. My passions drive me to work hard and occasionally greet me with success. For instance, just last week I got to sing at the Grand Ole Opry. Though I may have wasted a box of Pepto-bismol, my Pepto moment helped me discover my passions and gave me the drive and courage to pursue them to the best of my ability.

WHY YALE

What in particular about Yale has influenced your decision to apply?
(100 words or less)

I've wanted to attend Yale since the fourth grade and for the same reason that I want to attend now. I live in a community where education is put very low on the list of priorities. For most of my life I've sat bored in classrooms. I've been seeking the challenge that Yale would provide. I want to enrich my being at Yale while being surrounded by peers who are as passionate about learning as I am. With its liberal arts education, Yale also gives me the opportunity to continue being a well-rounded individual while pursuing the arts.

ADDITIONAL QUESTIONS

What excites you intellectually, really?
The fact that among billions of people and billions of years of life on this planet, my life and yours have somehow crossed paths. Human interaction amazes me because of the capabilities each interaction has for the individual and for our world.

Think about a disappointment you have experienced. What was your response?
I think that we sometimes fail and experience disappointment so that better opportunities can come our way. It's tough to be positive like this, but in hindsight this theory has proven true many times for me. I now tell myself: que sera sera.

Suite-style living may be an integral part of your Yale College experience. What would you contribute to the dynamic of your suite?
My friends often laugh at me and say I'm nerdy but still fun and cool. I would definitely bring enthusiasm and positive energy to the suite, but would also support, listen and help my peers if they're ever in need.

What do you wish you were better at being or doing?
Sometimes I wish I was more carefree. I'm a perfectionist and sometimes this negatively affects me. I often have remind myself of how enormous this universe is and how small my problems are in the bigger picture.

THE ROAD TO YALE

Chapter

9

Jonathan

PUBLIC HIGH SCHOOL
UNITED STATES

Public High School, U.S.

Freshman	Sophomore	Junior	Senior
Honors Freshman English	Honors Sophomore English	AP English Language	AP English Literature
Honors Pre-Calculus	AP Calculus BC	AP Statistics	AP Psychology
Biology	AP Biology	AP Chemistry	AP Physics C
Latin I	Latin II	Latin III	AP Latin IV
Honors Global Studies	AP World History	AP U.S. History	AP Macroeconomics
Health Education	Physics	AP Computer Science	AP Government and Politics
PE	Tennis	Tennis	Video Production

Before High School and Outside Classes

Honors Geometry

Honors Algebra II

Chemistry

Jonathan

EXTRACURRICULAR AND WORK EXPERIENCE

DECA, International Career Development Conference (11–12)
Mu Alpha Theta, Vice president (9–12)
Latin Club, President (9–12)
Piano, California State Panel Honors (K–12)
Science Olympiad, President (9–12)
Tennis, Varsity tennis (10–11)

SUMMER ACTIVITIES

Summer Science Program, New Mexico Tech (11)
Huazhong Agricultural University, China, Genetics intern (10)

AWARDS AND HONORS

Academics
National Merit Scholar (12)
Bay Area Science Olympiad, Designer Genes, First Place (11)
DECA International Career Development Conference, First Place (11)
Stanford Math Tournament, General Test, Third Place (11)
U.S. National Biology Olympiad, Semifinalist (10)
National Latin Exam, Gold and Silver Medals (9–11)

Performing Arts
U.S. Open Music Competition, Showcase Piano Solo Senior Division, Second Place (11)
California State Panel Honors for Piano (10)

COMMON APPLICATION ESSAY

Recount an incident or time when you experienced failure. How did it affect you, and what lessons did you learn? (250-650 words)

I jumped out of my seat and cheered, amazed by what I had just witnessed. Out of all the acts in the talent show, this one stood out to me by far: a contrast of violent jerks and fluidity that captured the music remarkably well. It was a form of urban dance called popping. Dancing was about the last thing I could imagine myself doing, but at that moment, I decided I was going to learn. It's really just a series of motions, I thought, and with a scientific and logical approach, it should be no problem. How hard can it be?

Once I reached home, I spent the remainder of the night analyzing videos of professional dancers and carefully observing how they moved. Okay, right foot here, knees slightly bent, left arm there angled sixty-two degrees at the elbow, palm facing parallel to the ground. A few hours of scrutiny later, I had what I thought to be an abundance of moves at my disposal. Arm wave, pindrop, glide, tut—I pieced together each individual move I had learned, preparing to create a physical concerto that would rival the magnificence of Rachmaninoff's Third. What resulted was closer to the work of a middle school orchestra that forgot to tune. My movements were disjointed and disharmonious, and I could only dance for seconds before exhausting everything I learned.

The order of the movements must be wrong, I thought. Maybe I should glide, pindrop, arm wave, and then tut? I tested every possible permutation, but each was as awkward as the last. Dumbfounded and unexpectedly tired, I collapsed onto my bed. What am I doing wrong? Maybe my movements aren't exact enough; after all, a minor error in measurement can drastically change the results of an experiment.

As I lay there pondering what to do, my mind began to drift to the music that still continued to play, unsympathetic to my failure. I heard the syncopated bass, the light snares, the subtle clicks—all the intricacies I hadn't given much attention to before. Soon, the music was all I could focus on. Every beat carried a small surge of energy, pushing me to get up. Despite my fatigue, the sound ultimately triumphed and brought me to my feet. My arms and legs moved as willed by the music, ignoring the textbook moves I had studied and creating their own variations instead. I simply watched in the mirror as a spectator, as if back in the chair at the talent show. With the last beat of the song, my body finally stopped. I stared at myself. I had just freestyled. It was far from what a dancer would consider good, but it was much more coherent than my first attempt. And most importantly, it felt good.

I had been trying to piece moves together when they didn't fit, like a baby trying to cram the circle piece down the square hole. Really, dancing is not the rigid puzzle that I thought it was; the pieces are fluid, and I can morph them to fit one another in the way I want. Though the urban dance may look robotic, the mindset behind it is much more free and creative, visually outlining the texture of a beat. Without a doubt, the moves I learned by analyzing those videos helped me greatly, but they served only as the foundation for my intuition to build upon. Analytical thinking on its own isn't always enough. Sometimes I just need to follow my gut when a dose of inspiration comes along.

The following year, I decided to dance at the same talent show. As the audience roared and I walked off the stage, many friends asked where on earth I had learned those moves.

"I didn't. They were in me all along."

They told me to cut the fairy tale crap and just tell them.

SUPPLEMENTAL ESSAY

In this essay, please reflect on something you would like us to know about you that we might not learn from the rest of your application, or on something about which you would like to say more. You may write about anything—from personal experiences or interests to intellectual pursuits. (500 words or less)

"There's the constellation Hercules. See? There's his body, and his arms go up that way."

I squinted and tried to follow where my roommate Jake was pointing. The sky was cloudless and the moon was only a dim crescent, allowing the stars to shine brilliantly. I hardly knew anything about astronomy before coming to the Summer Science Program, or SSP; the subject was almost never mentioned in school and the light pollution at home made the night sky relatively bland and uninspiring. Here in the New Mexican desert, however, I was far from city lights and could view the stars in their full glory.

Jake knew every constellation, the names of nearly every visible star, and the locations of every major galaxy. Meanwhile, I wasn't even sure where Mars was. While I struggled with the astronomy problems, he thought they were a breeze, and he taught me whatever I didn't understand in lecture. He was the expert in the observatory. In the computer lab, however, he was not as comfortable. He had no prior experience with programming, and I was glad to help him debug his code whenever he had trouble.

The assignments at SSP were more challenging than any I had ever experienced before, and the difficulty of the research was literally astronomical—we were tracking an asteroid and calculating its orbit. Nobody walked out of the lecture room understanding everything. We all caught just snippets, and only after putting our collective knowledge together could we begin to understand the material necessary for our research.

Although we were at what we affectionately called "nerd camp," there was an incredible amount of diversity in tastes, beliefs, and talents. My peers constantly inspired me not only through their different approaches to a problem, but also through their varied opinions and experiences. Collaboration to such an extent was new to me, and it allowed me to see from many new perspectives that I otherwise could not have found on my own. SSP would have been impossible to complete alone.

"Do you know where Orion is?" I asked Jake. I had heard about the mythological figure before and was curious what the constellation looked like.

"Oh, that's a winter constellation. We can't see it now in the summer. But hey, at least you'll see it eventually. The southern constellations, like Crux, are never visible in the northern hemisphere at any time of the year."

I found that a bit disappointing, but also quite humbling. Some stars can only ever be seen from certain locations, and each location on Earth offers a different perspective of the sky. To learn about all the stars around us, then, people all over the world need to share data and work together. What we were doing at SSP wasn't really much different.

WHY YALE

What in particular about Yale has influenced your decision to apply?
(100 words or less)

Small and big schools both have their pros and cons, but Yale offers the best of both worlds. Yale's residential college system allows for the tightly-knit community that I find important. The liberal arts environment gives undergraduates enough attention, yet Yale still retains the world-class research opportunities and connections unavailable at a small school. Yale also offers a multitude of extracurricular activities that I'm sure I would enjoy. After talking with some friends who are alumni or current students at Yale, I have been convinced that Yale and I would be a great fit.

ADDITIONAL QUESTIONS

What excites you intellectually, really?
Seeing mathematical calculations apply to the physical world is exciting. It's amazing that the ancient Greeks got a close estimate of the Earth's circumference without using any fancy equipment, only the shadows and some geometry.

Think about a disappointment you have experienced. What was your response?
I was looking forward to singing in my school's chamber choir after I got in, but I was forced to drop the class because it was during the same period as AP Latin. Although I can't sing in choir, I still sing with my friends outside school for fun.

Suite-style living may be an integral part of your Yale College experience. What would you contribute to the dynamic of your suite?
I would be the guy that my suite mates occasionally have to tell to keep it down. I might be playing music and cracking jokes, or I might be discussing anything from the fundamental questions of philosophy to the latest pop culture.

What do you wish you were better at being or doing?
I wish I was better with directions. I have lived in this town for pretty much my whole life, but I still have trouble getting around without a GPS. I do know where the nearest Chipotle is, though!

THE ROAD TO YALE

Chapter

10

Katie

PRIVATE HIGH SCHOOL
UNITED STATES

Private High School, U.S.

Freshman	Sophomore	Junior	Senior
English 9	English 10	English 11	English 12
Honors Math	Honors Algebra II	Honors Pre-Calculus	AP Calculus BC
World History	European History	AP U.S. History	AP Chemistry
Latin	Latin	AP Latin (Virgil)	Latin Lyric
Spanish	Spanish	AP Physics B	Studio Photography
Biology	Chemistry	Studio Photography	
Photography	Photography	Public Speaking	
	Music Appreciation*		
	Art History*		

* Asterisked classes are one-semester classes.

Katie

EXTRACURRICULAR AND WORK EXPERIENCE

Arts Board, Class representative (11–12)
Literary magazine, Arts editor (11–12)
School newspaper, Editor-in-chief (9–12)
Varsity Dance, Choreographer, dancer (9–12)
Yearbook, Photo editor (12)

SUMMER ACTIVITIES

Fundamental Photographs, Intern (11)
Mei Tao Photography, Intern (11)
Mount Sinai Hospital, Research intern (10)
Sino Language Program, Beijing, English teacher (9)

AWARDS AND HONORS

National Merit Scholar (12)
Annual Mathematics Award (11)
Annual Photography Award (11)
Cum Laude Society (11)
Edna Hill Robillard Award (11)
Scholastic Art & Writing Awards, Photography, Gold Key (11)
Annual Latin Award (10)
Annual Spanish Award (10)
Annual English Award (9)
National Spanish Examination, Second Place (9)
National Latin Examination, Summa Cum Laude (9–11)

COMMON APPLICATION ESSAY
Topic of your choice (250-650 words)

I see a photo I want to take. Without thinking I reach for my camera but my hands grasp only air. My fingers itch and ache as I stand in the middle of the street, pressing an imaginary shutter and muttering to myself. "Don't worry," I want to say to the stranger staring at me. "I'm not crazy, just a photographer without her camera."

I'm terrified of not having memories. I make lists of the week's highlights; I write down funny lines and conversations where I smiled like a fool the whole time because I was so deliriously happy. Photography feeds my need to record everything before my sleep-deprived mind forgets. These tangible objects help shape the narrative of my life, making each adventure in the park or expedition through the city unique. Photos aren't frozen snapshots of time, but rather living, breathing moments. I can look at a photo and relive the bliss of finding some sunlight on a winter day or the exhilaration of wandering through a magical forest on the outskirts of Beijing.

My photography reflects my interests, my fascinations, my obsessions. I can't resist minimalist lines and shadows, be they in a well-designed airport or a public art installation. I have enough photos of my friend Katie to wallpaper a mansion, but I keep finding a new expression or pose that has me reaching for the camera. My New York is thousands of shots stitched together, forming the story of where I live and where I explore. There's the dancing girl in Washington Square Fountain, a red stoop in Chinatown where Katie and I took self-portraits, and a rooftop on the West Side where two daredevils climbed a water tower while I snapped away.

Photography allows me to show others how I see the world, yes. It's also how I remember that the world is worth seeing. There's something special even in my all-too-familiar neighborhood or school building, like the glint of a chandelier against the blue dusk or a heart-shaped leaf ten seconds from crumbling off its branch. I take the same route to and from school every day, but I still meander home with a camera swinging from my shoulder, looking for the next alluring shadow or window reflection to pull me in. I frame my life as I want to see it, with possibilities and potential galore.

Someone once asked if taking photos was my therapy. I misunderstood him and thought he was suggesting therapy as an alternative to photography. He was right, of course. I stress about finishing my art portfolio on time, sacrifice sleep to tape photos on my wall, and take forever to finish my homework because I'm also on Photoshop. But photography challenges my mind in a way nothing else does. There are no assignments in art, beyond the need to be honest to my vision. I set the questions—what excites me, what intrigues me, what impacts me—and I attempt to find the answers every time I look through the viewfinder.

SUPPLEMENTAL ESSAY
In this essay, please reflect on something you would like us to know about you that we might not learn from the rest of your application, or on something about which you would like to say more. You may write about anything—from personal experiences or interests to intellectual pursuits. (500 words or less)

"WE WANT AP CHEM. (please)"

The beseeching sign adorned the door to the chem lab. Many passersby were understandably confused—AP Chemistry is reputed to be the only class that makes you cry here (lies: AP Physics made me cry first), and its tests are legendary. But any former AP Chem student will only laugh knowingly. Because along with terrifying tests are the water fights, therapy sessions, and explosions that make the pain worth it. And one man is the source of all this madness.

Phillips is a classic mad scientist, with the bushy gray hair, mustache, and beard for the role. He is snarky, insulting, and bluntly honest. He gleefully makes fun of a student's ineptitude at printing lab reports on time, shamelessly teases someone about a summer crush, and threatens anti-curves when we do too well on tests. His brusque and sardonic "And your point is?" is a challenge to students, especially for those masochistic ones who enjoy making him care. Because behind the sarcasm, there exists a human being who laughs at his students' jokes, consoles them when they come to him in tears, and gives bear hugs at the right moments.

When Phillips announced my junior year that he was applying for a sabbatical and might be away my senior year, it was unfathomable. To whom would I rant about the dark underbelly of humanity when no one sent me her newspaper articles in on time? Who would listen to my babbling about the travails of printing the yearbook in color?

Who would take me by the shoulders and tell me to stop stressing about things outside my control?

Phillips has no patience for indecision or feminine qualifiers. To get his attention I had to make a statement. I reminded Phillips of my grade's absurdly high chem average in sophomore year, preached the joys of AP Chem to my classmates, and littered the science laboratories with signs begging for the class. My crusade became a running joke at school. I had no say in whether he would get his sabbatical, but you can't say I didn't try.

As much as I love stoichiometry and redox reactions, the potential lack of AP Chem wasn't the only problem. I couldn't imagine senior year without Phillips's sarcasm, advice that makes me cry, or reminders to take care of myself first. He is one of those rare adults who listen. He takes my opinions seriously and taught me to speak up for myself (which he might've regretted when I protested his sabbatical). Phillips has questioned and challenged me until I can offer airtight arguments, and I've learned from him how to be critical of things in a thoughtful yet biting way, a handy skill in life.

Phillips postponed his sabbatical for several reasons, my fervent campaign probably being low on the list. AP Chem is as challenging as promised, but I go to class knowing this was something I begged, pleaded, and cajoled my way into. After brutal tests, I think of the alternative—a year without the insults, pranks, and honesty I've come to love.

WHY YALE?

What in particular about Yale has influenced your decision to apply?
(100 words or less)

What I love about Yale is the contrast between the cohesiveness of the residential college system and the multifaceted nature of the larger university. Attending a small school within New York City closely mirrors this dynamic. Everyone I met at Yale was invested in their communities, be it their Directed Studies class, residential college, or acapella group. I thrive when I have the freedom to explore my intellectual and creative passions and would love to do so at Yale.

ADDITIONAL QUESTIONS

What would you do with a free afternoon tomorrow?
I would go on an adventure with friends and bring my camera along with me.

What is the best piece of advice you have received in the last three years?
Speak up! The toughest boss I've ever had (affectionately nicknamed Tiger Boss by me) intimidated me so much I often didn't speak my mind with her. But that was exactly what frustrated her the most. She has never been afraid to stand up for herself, and she wanted me to do exactly the same.

If you could witness one moment in history, what would it be and why?
I'd witness the Big Bang to grasp the awesomeness (in the original meaning of awesome) of an event outside of my possible perception.

What do you wish you were better at being or doing?
I wish I was better at dancing, in order to fall into that suspension of thought and total flow of movement and physical control that happens in a great dance, with a great dancer.

What is something about which you have changed your mind in the last three years?
New York has grown and shrunk (figuratively, although perhaps physically too) in the last three years. I used to think my future and my life could be contained in the bustling madness of this city, but now I'm eyeing other cities, other states, even other countries, and wondering where I'll end up.

THE ROAD TO YALE

Chapter

11

Kayla

PUBLIC HIGH SCHOOL
UNITED STATES

Public High School, U.S.

Freshman	Sophomore	Junior	Senior
Honors Freshman English	Honors Sophomore English	AP English Language	AP English Literature
Honors Geometry	Honors Algebra II/ Trigonometry	Honors Pre-Calculus	AP Calculus BC
Honors Biology	Honors Chemistry	AP Chemistry	AP Biology
AP World History	AP U.S. History	AP U.S. History	AP Physics
Spanish II	Honors Spanish III	AP Spanish IV	AP Government/ We the People Team
Computer Applications*	Advanced Women's Choir	AP Psychology	AP Microeconomics
Lincoln–Douglas Debate	Honors Lincoln–Douglas Debate	Advanced Women's Choir	Women's Glee
Math Theory (math team)	Honors Math Theory	Honors Math Theory	Honors Math Theory
Improvisation*			

Before High School and Outside Classes

Spanish I

* Asterisked classes are one-semester classes.

Kayla

EXTRACURRICULARS AND WORK EXPERIENCE

Choir, President (10–12)
Christian church youth group, Youth social chair, worship team leader, singer, guitarist, pianist (7–12)
High school math team (9–12)
Kumon Math and Reading Center, Grader and data entry (11–12)
Lincoln–Douglas Debate (9–10)
Pianist, Church pianist (7–12)
Tornado Relief Book Drive Project, Founder, director (10)
Research intern (11–12)
Varsity Mock Trial team attorney (12)
We the People Team (11–12)

SUMMER ACTIVITIES

University, Research intern (11–12)
Summer mission trips (9–10)

AWARDS AND HONORS

TX YIG state convention, qualified for National Judicial Competition (Major League), Third Place (12)
Girls State Delegate (12)
National Honor Society (12)
National Merit Scholar (12)
U.S. National Chemistry Olympiad, Semifinalist (11)
We the People, Team Competitor State Champions, National Top Five Team (11)
Lincoln–Douglas Debate, State semifinalist (10)

COMMON APPLICATION ESSAY

Describe a place or environment where you are perfectly content. What do you do or experience there, and why is it meaningful to you? (250-650 words)

Sound. Beautiful, harmonic sound echoes within the bare, beige walls of my basement. The old, upright Yamaha, its keys yellowing with use, stands like a grand Carnegie Hall Steinway. The worn, acoustic guitar sits in its sacred corner, its six strings coaxing me to play. Although these two simple instruments are all that furnish the unembellished room, this underground sanctuary holds my buried treasure—music.

Strum. Pedal. Sing. The lifestyle that gives me breath. I hum by day, karaoke by night, and opera by shower.

I dig through Beethoven, Chopin, and Mozart. It's a difficult choice, but today I am feeling the Romantic Period. I pick up my favorite Chopin nocturne and let myself forget the Western Blots waiting at the research lab, the Books for tornado relief donations waiting to be sorted, the ice cream waiting in the freezer. Instead, I indulge myself in the nocturne until I am no longer in my little room but floating romantically across a serene lake glistening under the moonlight. From the first grace note to the final chord, I am lost in a midnight world of E minor.

I love playing music, but creating music? That is my eternal, burning passion. I am not a performer, but I am an original. I live not for impressions but for authenticity—and that is reflected in the way music is created in my sanctuary. My musical solitude engenders the enchantment of hearing the hollow guitar body echo my strums and feeling the piano keys vibrate under my touch. I conjure up accompaniments and twist existing songs. I compose pieces and write lyrics about anything my heart fancies—love, tragedy, life, food. Each time I create a line or a melody, I become closer to myself. Every new song and new chord adds a little more internal peace, a little more enlightened soul.

In my frenzy of crumpled sheet music, late night compositions, and rock-hard finger calluses, I found another welcoming instrument: the human voice. As an avid vocalist and a notorious hummer, singing amazes me. What voices are capable of! Head voice can be polished with vibrato, and falsetto can be transformed with riffs and runs. Harmonizing brings the cheerleader, yearbook editor, and science geek (like I am) together. An a capella group, once an assembly of strangers, stands in a circle of different faces and different interests, but in a moment of harmony we are a family. Each singer's voice and energy are essential to the symphony, my soprano balanced by neighboring altos. And when we open our mouths to fill the silence... how wonderful the sound!

I can harmonize traditional African songs with my a cappella group. I can pick up the guitar and write a song about a boy crush like Taylor Swift. I can play Beethoven and travel to the Classical Period. I can do anything. So as I lose myself in my beloved underground kingdom, I am comforted to know that here I am the queen and the servant, the artist and the audience, the silence and the music. Where there is musical harmony, there is a certain beauty that cannot be described without a certain joy and a certain magic. And the magic is all right here—in the notes, in the chords, and in the musician.

SUPPLEMENTAL ESSAY

If you selected one of the engineering majors, please write a brief essay telling us what has led you to an interest in this field of study, what experiences (if any) you have had in engineering, and what it is about Yale's engineering program that appeals to you. (500 words or less)

From a young age, I have always been fascinated by science, mathematics, and technology—the random, the rules, the real. I have explored various subjects, experimenting from periodic elements to problem solving to cancer research, always searching for that one passion to settle with. I did not fall in love with biomedical engineering gradually or intentionally. Rather, it was the second month of my university internship, just a normal day at the research lab. I was using an Olympus fluorescence microscope to examine an immunofluorescence staining on cancer cells. As I was taking photographs of the glowing cell protein, and as the lens focused on the piercing blue nuclei, an overwhelming feeling of wonder struck me. Someone found how to make these chemicals attach to cell structures and glow. Someone created this powerful microscope to view tiny shades of certain light wavelengths. And now, I am using these mind-blowing innovations to discover the human body. When I reflect on how the laws of the physical, the chemical, and the living can work together, curiosity completely consumes me. Often times, we research enthusiasts, engrossed in our own experiments, fail to remember how fascinating the lab equipment is. How a Western Blot, after putting protein through thousands of centrifuge spins and gels and electric charges and milk and antibodies and horseradish peroxidase and oodles of lab jargon, ends with a line of bands on a piece of film, telling me if I am on the road to curing cancer or not—that is amazing. I dream of innovating technology—from bioimaging to synthetic biomaterials—that will save lives and help future scientists all over the world, but first I want to know more, much more. And I want to know more at Yale.

Yale's Biomedical Engineering program, though fairly young, has contributed extraordinary breakthroughs. Not only has the research completely wowed me, but the whole incorporation of Yale undergraduates into the department and the support from the faculty highly appeals to me. Fusing engineering with clinical medicine to make an impact in both human health and scientific advancement is my dream, and I would love to join Yale's exceptional engineers in discovery and innovation. After learning about the School, the question I ask is no longer why Yale Biomedical Engineering, but why not? This is how I want to impact the world with my resources—with what I know, what I will learn, and what I can discover—in engineering and medicine. This is what I treasure and always will.

WHY YALE

What in particular about Yale has influenced your decision to apply?
(100 words or less)

Aside from the outstanding engineering program and brilliant professors (like Professor Akhil Reed Amar, whose work and zeal for the Constitution are an inspiration to me), I have been especially won over by the Yale community. The student body encompasses a special atmosphere of comradeship and joy and humor that makes me say, "Wow. This is the place I want to call home." From Freshman Move-in Day to Harry Potter housing, from shopping week to Master's Tea to graduating wearing the headgear of one's choice, my wish is for Yale traditions to one day become my traditions.

ADDITIONAL QUESTIONS

What excites you intellectually, really?
The unknown. The nothingness that space is expanding into, the technology of the future, the cures yet to save lives. It is the knowledge that my generation will one day discover the unknown of today that truly thrills me.

Think about a disappointment you have experienced. What was your response?
At Girls State, I lost runoff elections after the impassioned campaigns and debates. Although initially disheartened, what I gained through the trial—knowledge, stamina, friendship, and a passion for government—empowered me with confidence.

Suite-style living may be an integral part of your Yale College experience. What would you contribute to the dynamic of your suite?
At 2 am on Saturday, I would either be creating a spontaneous a cappella circle or philosophizing about the universe with my fellow suitemates over ice cream. I would be a bond, a bridge, a sister.

What do you wish you were better at being or doing?
I wish to be a better scientist and friend. Advancing knowledge changes the world; being a true friend changes lives. To me, there is no limit to science or friendship. I will always strive to grow in both.

THE ROAD TO YALE

Chapter

12

Lourdes

**PRIVATE HIGH SCHOOL
UNITED STATES**

Private High School, U.S.

Freshman	Sophomore	Junior	Senior
Intro Literature	Composition and Literature	Landscape Literature	Honors Romanticism, Modernism and Postmodernism
Honors Algebra II	Intensive Writing	Honors Research Methods	AP Statistics
Honors Physics	Honors World History	Honors Biology	AP Microeconomics
Honors World Geography	Spanish II	Honors Ecology	AP U.S. History
Spanish I	Honors Chemistry	Honors Environmental Ethics	Spanish III
Intro Visual Study	Chemistry Lab	Honors Environmental Project	AP Environmental Science
Lab/Physics	Pre-Calculus, AP Calculus AB	Honors Nature Photography	Honors Monetary Theory
Symphony Orchestra	World History	AP Calculus AB	Honors Constitutional Law
World Religions			Honors Sustainable International Development: Food for Thought Advanced

Lourdes

EXTRACURRICULAR AND WORK EXPERIENCE

Chamber orchestra (9)

Christian Fellowship, Youth leader (9–12)

Cross country (6–9)

Congressman Gary Holder-Winfield (D-CT) Campaign, Intern, fellow (10)

Friends of Nature (Chinese environmental NGO), Translator, member (9, 11)

International Student Society, Co-founder, vice president (9–12)

JV and Varsity Basketball, Co-captain (11–12)

KEC Outreach Group, Founder (11–12)

Spearmint, Environmental NGO, Founder, president (10–12)

United Nations Environmental Program TUNZA, Eco-generation Regionals Ambassador for China (12)

Violin (3–12)

Yale Center for Environmental Law and Policy, Research assistant (11–12)

SUMMER ACTIVITIES

Shanghai Normal University, Research and writing assistant (11)

Charyou (Chinese environmental start-up), Design intern (9)

Dacheng Law Firm, Intern (9)

Friends of Nature, Volunteer (8)

Stepping Stone Organization, English teaching assistant (7)

Hands On Shanghai (Shanghai Children's Hospital charity), Intern (9–12)

AWARDS AND HONORS

President's Volunteer Service Award (12)

Prudential Spirit of Community Award (12)

International Young Eco-Hero Award (11)

National AP Scholar (11)

NextGenVest National Educational Business Script Competition, Third Place (11)

National Merit, Semifinalist (11)

Dean's List (9–12)

High school Sesame Seed Grant (10–11)

COMMON APPLICATION ESSAY

Some students have a background or story so central to their identity that they believe their application would be incomplete without it. (250-650 words)

Kindling the Green Flame

After returning home from a stressful day at school, I scowled at my reflection in the dusty bathroom mirror. Red lines ran around my cheeks and nose, marks from a newly acquired contraption—my particulate mask.

Our relationship began in the summer of 2008. Following my parents' job relocation, I moved from a pristine Pennsylvania suburb to Shanghai. Stepping out of the Shanghai airport, I took my first breath. A single thought-this air tastes horrible! In America, I had enjoyed nature's beauty; hiding in the bushes to watch baby deer, climbing birch trees to follow squirrels, and watching crimson sunsets from my front porch were my childhood pastimes. My naïve ten-year-old mind could only think of how the concrete jungle that was Shanghai would foil my future outdoor fun.

The situation was more serious than I thought. During my first summer in Shanghai, I caught a chronic cold from inhaling the particulate matter my air conditioning unit pumped into my room each day. My doctor told me the unexpected environment change had caught my immune system "off guard." I began wearing a particulate mask, and, soon, my sickness disappeared.

When I overheard classmates also complain about the air quality, I eagerly promoted my survival secret to them, only to win their scoffs. I began to hope that improving my environment would protect me from future illness and-more importantly at the time- from losing my friends' respect.

When the 2010 Expo ushered in a cleaner Shanghai, my interest in addressing Shanghai's pollution grew more complex. New government policies requiring fuel-efficient taxis, electric buses, and the shutdown of polluting factories had reduced the

amount of particulate matter in the air. New government initiatives also taught citizens how to live green by recycling. Finally, marathoners could run without contracting lung infections or tripping over plastic bags! But, after the Expo closed, I watched in dismay as the sky darkened by shades of grey and citizens began to litter again. Intrigued by the power of policy, I pored over government and economics books at the library to discover with excitement that with the passing of a well-devised policy, the government could drastically improve citizens' lives. I began to dream of a life in public service. Though I did not join the Chinese government, I joined several non-governmental environmental organizations (NGOs) based in Shanghai to help improve my city's environmental situation.

As I spread environmental awareness with NGOs, I realized that my childhood education and experiences in nature formed the basis of my commitment to the environment. If Chinese youth would determine the future of China's environment, why weren't organizations appealing to them? An idea struck me: I'd create my *own* Chinese environmental education organization for youth around the world. Using the resources of my American school, my group led two citywide trash cleanups in two years that have touched the lives of millions of students and adults through the media. Now, in the U.S., my previous experience in China drives my efforts to spread environmental awareness at my school through blogging, Conservation Proctors, and my Kohler Environmental Center outreach group, because my classmates, too, will determine the fate of the Earth.

In forming my organization, I realized that the process of discovering solutions to issues I encounter brings me joy. Whether proposing policy solutions in academic research, devising a plan of implementation for a new environmental initiative, or figuring out how to puncture the defense on the court, the challenge of digging past superficial understanding and making appropriate plans delights me as much as the outcome. Now, I'm ready to tackle my future. When the smog thickens and new trials arise in my life, I will strap on my particulate mask and advance forward, an agent for change.

SUPPLEMENTAL ESSAY

In this essay, please reflect on something you would like us to know about you that we might not learn from the rest of your application, or on something about which you would like to say more. You may write about anything—from personal experiences or interests to intellectual pursuits. (500 words or less)

After climbing four flights of stairs in the sticky Tianjin heat, I swung open the door to my aunt's cool apartment. She was pudgier than I remembered. She attempted to sit up to hug me but couldn't, so she settled on flashing a warm smile in my direction. My own smile masked my confusion.

"*Da yi ma?*" I asked.

"*Da yi ma* has multiple sclerosis (MS)," my mom explained quickly. The more I gazed at my aunt's feeble body, the more a suffocating feeling of dread rose in my chest.

Was she dying?

I scarcely believed that *Da yi ma*'s situation could worsen since my visit last year. At that time, she could only pay her apartment rent with help from my parents. But, to my surprise, *Da yi ma* found new ways to cultivate her own happiness. To celebrate Chinese New Year, she bought a one-dollar red-eared slider turtle. Lifting her companion out of his dull metal pot, she smirked as he ran in circles on the tile floor. She also poked fun at me when I attempted—unsuccessfully—to prevent him from getting stuck under the couch. Summer adventures with my aunt made me wonder if I could ever experience this simple happiness in my American life.

After internalizing the concept of the American dream as a young girl, I wondered if *Da yi ma*'s happiness was faked. My definition of happiness revolved around receiving stickers on my homework and falling asleep to the sound of rain in my parents' SUV. My aunt was not pursuing happiness through her achievement or material goods. So, how could she be truly happy? How could anyone with MS be happy?

Ironically, my experience in America challenged my American dream. At boarding school, I met others who believed happiness could result only from success. Some chased success so vigorously that they neglected to appreciate the moment. I soon realized that achievement only led to short-lived happiness. By observing how little MS seemed to restrain *Da yi ma*'s joy, I decided that if I lived life the best I could, I deserved to be happy.

Nine years later, news of *Da yi ma*'s death reached me. I could not bear to use her name in conversation for several weeks. In my vigilant silence, her unusually steadfast love for life inspired me to view "the pursuit of happiness" from a different perspective.

I now consider "pursuit of happiness" a misnomer. Instead, "cultivating happiness" is my choice phrase. Following my aunt's legacy, I've learned to cultivate my appreciation of the present: I rejoice when I see the bright grins of children after a volunteer music concert and enjoy discussing the complex personality of Emily Bronte's Heathcliff. Today, though I continue striving toward my goals, my love for life itself—not solely the fruits of labor—gives me true happiness. With *Da yi ma*'s spirit in my heart, I'm optimistic about my future; no fall will ever crush my dreams.

WHY YALE

What in particular about Yale has influenced your decision to apply?
(100 words or less)

Yale undergraduates' intellectual depth, passion, and entrepreneurial spirit impress me. The insightfulness of undergraduates who taught Choate debaters sparked my curiosity for logical thinking and my academic interests—government, economics, and social activism. The passion of undergraduate activists I saw while attending Yale's student-run Asian American Leadership conference inspired me to work towards being a more persuasive social and environmental activist. I saw at the student-run Yale Food Systems Symposium that, with Yale's resources, self-starters like Yale undergraduates and myself could change our future. Through a Yale education, I am free to develop the traits of the undergraduates whom I admire.

ADDITIONAL QUESTIONS

What excites you intellectually, really?
The intersections between forms of social oppression, particularly the relationship between the oppressed and their environment, fascinate me. Through study, I could understand how to address global oppression through policy, economics, or advocacy.

Think about a disappointment you have experienced. What was your response?
My dream of serving my community through Student Council was crushed when I lost the election. I proposed a new election process through Choate's newspaper and discovered editorials and Conservation Proctors were equally effective ways to contribute.

Suite-style living may be an integral part of your Yale College experience. What would you contribute to the dynamic of your suite?
I'd offer my fair-trade 80% cacao chocolate to new friends. I'd join in their fun, and they'd join me in pick-up basketball, making dumplings, and group reading. I'd listen, challenge their perspectives, and encourage free inquiry as means to growth.

What do you wish you were better at being or doing?
I could develop my sense of humor and my ability to relax others around me more.

THE ROAD TO YALE

Chapter

13

Nini

PUBLIC HIGH SCHOOL
UNITED STATES

Public High School, U.S.

Freshman	Sophomore	Junior	Senior
Geometry	Honors Algebra 2	Honors Pre-Calculus	AP Calculus BC
Honors English 1	Honors English 2	Honors English 3	AP English Language
French 2	Honors French 3	AP French 4	AP Statistics
Honors Biology 1	AP Chemistry 2	AP Biology 2	Graphic Design
Honors World History	AP European History	AP Physics B	AP Physics C
AP Psychology	AP Computer Science	AP U.S. History	Advanced Computer Science Project

Before High School and Outside Classes

Honors Chemistry	Economics
French 1	American Government

Nini

EXTRACURRICULAR AND WORK EXPERIENCE

Ballroom dance, Latin Dance competitor (6–12)

China–U.S. Medical Science Conference, Translator, interpreter (10–12)

Disabled Youth for Figure Skating, Volunteer, assistant coach (8–12)

Figure skating, Singles National Competitor (1–12)

National Science Honors Society, Treasurer (11–12)

Scientific research (7–12)

Tutor Doctor, Inc., Tutor (11–12)

Tests of Engineering Aptitude, Mathematics and Science, President (9–12)

United States Figure Skating Association, Special Program for Teaching Mentally Disabled Youth for Figure Skating (8–12)

SUMMER ACTIVITIES

120 Beijing Emergency Medical Center, Assistant paramedic, volunteer (11)

Chinese Academy of Sciences Institute of Biophysics, Intern (11)

California State Summer School for Mathematics and Science, Participant (10)

California Youth Science Summer Camp, University of California, San Francisco, Counselor (10)

Irvine Stem Cell Research Center, University of California, Volunteer (9)

AWARDS AND HONORS

Academics

California State Science Fair, Pharmacology and Toxicology, Second Place (11)

Los Angeles County Science Fair, Biochemistry, Honorable Mention (11)

Society of In Vitro Biology, Outstanding Achievement for Ability and Creativity (11)

Tests of Engineering Aptitude, Mathematics and Science, First Place (10–11)

President's Volunteer Service Award, Gold (9–12)

PVPUSD District Science Fair, Biochemistry, First Place (10–12)

Model United Nations, Multiple awards (9–11)

Athletics

United States Figure Skating Association, National Showcase, Second Place (9–12)

COMMON APPLICATION ESSAY

Some students have a background or story so central to their identity that they believe their application would be incomplete without it. (250-650 words)

SUKI

My cousin Suki's first car was pale pink in color, furnished with Hello Kitty rugs and seat covers, featuring a nearly naked baby boy bobbing its head on the dashboard and a pair of plush pandas where others hung dice. It was simultaneously the most exciting and terrifying experience to ride in her car; Suki drove the dainty vehicle like a tank with liberal use of her horn. In the chaos of Beijing traffic, she had maneuvered the car through countless near accidents and maybe some accidents. I once questioned her choice of vehicle and she retorted, with her characteristic sass:

"You can decide what car I drive when you buy me one."

Last summer, I returned to China for the first time in four years, and the first thing I did when I got off the plane was see Suki. When she saw me, rather than her usual cheeky greeting expressing false concern at my lack of growth, Suki burst into tears.

I watched my second sister blubbering on the hospital bed and froze, the insanity of the change that had taken place in these few years overwhelming me with regret. The Suki I left four years prior had been voluptuous in size and personality, but the Suki that greeted me now was half her previous weight and sobbing with an unfamiliar pain. The stroke she had at age 33 left the right side of her body near useless and dimmed the charm and confidence she had before. I wanted to comfort her like she comforted me when I fell asleep on a dance stage. I wanted to scream at the cause of her pain like she screamed at the neighborhood boy who pushed me over while roller blading. Most of all, I wanted to hug her, and tell her that her life was not defined by disease, that she was perfect as she was, like she had done when I cried over the embarrassment of my eczema.

It was terrifying to see someone so strong, someone who taught me to be me, become so fragile looking. Nonetheless, I sat down on her bed as her crying grew softer, and started to talk. I told her about how I had beat my eczema, how I no longer let my embarrassment stop me from doing what I wanted. I told her about how she inspired me to research stroke, how someday I could help her roller skate again. She finally stopped crying and her lips formed into a slight, rueful smile.

"You've finally grown up." She choked out.

I returned to Suki's room every few days that month. On some days, I was her personal trainer, narrating her slow recovery of her joints with growing intensity and drama.

Other days, we simply sang our hearts out with the aid of a rickety karaoke machine.

On the day of my flight back home, I visited Suki's room for the last time, stopping to glance at the car parked outside. I saw now that it wore this shade of pink with confidence in its uniqueness and abilities. It was simultaneously soft in the interior yet tough to its core, able to continue functioning despite any accident or scrape, unapologetically peculiar and inarguably charismatic. Suki chose a car that was, or rather, is herself. As I grew up with the memories of her in her car, the driver and the personality of the ride had transformed from Suki, into me. I had inadvertently soaked up the strength and personality she radiated during even her lowest times.

As I waved goodbye to my cousin for the year, she looked at me with eyes brimming with the fire I thought she'd lost, and stated with her characteristic sass:

"When you discover the cure for stroke, you damn better name it after me".

"I will."

SUPPLEMENTAL ESSAY

In this essay, please reflect on something you would like us to know about you that we might not learn from the rest of your application, or on something about which you would like to say more. You may write about anything—from personal experiences or interests to intellectual pursuits. (500 words or less)

When my older sister was born in Los Angeles, my grandmother was elated. She pushed forward her kidney stone surgery with dogged determination to make a flight the next day. In China, because of the sheer number of patients and the desperate lack of medical practitioners, the first to be treated are the ones who have extra money to offer, who can surreptitiously slip a red pouch of money to the doctor. The intern, in charge because the primary doctor received one such pouch, believed the heart monitor to be malfunctioning when it recorded strange, erratic patterns. It wasn't the monitor. It was my grandma jolted by a sudden heart attack. She passed away on November 15, 1993, less than 16 hours after my sister was born.

I have seen these malfeasances personally during my internship on a Beijing emergency ambulance: a hospital discharging a penniless homeless man who had fallen from a two-story building and an ambulance that quickly U-turned when another caller phoned, promising an extra red pouch for speed. I never knew what happened to the first man, the initially injured caller whose ambulance never arrived, or even my Grandma Lee, but I know the residual pain that affects those that are left behind, like my mother. Her blanched expression and reddened eyes every year on my sister's birthday communicate pain and anger. I know the distant look that my grandpa gets when he looks at me and sees his wife of fifty years. I know what he hopes for when he asks me again if I am a doctor yet.

His question prompted me to volunteer at a doctor's office, where I got my first real glimpse into the world of medicine. As a neurologist, Dr. Bharadia got an eclectic sampling of patients, from the garrulous grandma with Alzheimer's to the reticent toddler with insomnia. But no matter what the character or affliction, she treated all with unwavering attention, gleaning as much information as possible, using a dictionary to translate Spanish if necessary, and always, no matter the size of her workload, rechecking the facts of her patients to make sure they received the best diagnosis possible. She was a doctor who was driven by the warmth of a smile rather than the chill of the coin, and her influence resonated.

I have been offered a rare and fortuitous glance at the many sides of the medical die: the domestic and the international, the selfishness and selflessness, the actions of the practitioner and the reactions of the patient. But throughout the good and the bad experiences, my desire to heal and to fix has only swelled. This doesn't necessarily mean a doctor of medicine, but also a doctor of injustice who cures the diseases plaguing health care.

My grandpa still asks me every year if I am a doctor yet. The answer is yes, in the most basic sense of the word; I am someone who heals small injustices today, and large injustices tomorrow.

WHY YALE

What in particular about Yale has influenced your decision to apply?
(100 words or less)

Last year, at Yale's Baker's Dozen A Capella concert at my school, I watched thirteen men belt out "Sunday Morning" with unexpected zest and euphonious energy. Yale had been simply a word with vague connotations of prestige and success, but seeing this camaraderie, immaculate in blazers, slacks and blazing smiles, humanized Yale. I'm applied to a school in which hearty academics are supplemented by genuine passions, academic or otherwise, and an earnest community. Yale has medical students who protest socioeconomic inequality with Die-ins, who challenge professors on abuse policies, who learn not simply to learn, but to defend their beliefs.

ADDITIONAL QUESTIONS

What excites you intellectually, really?

Learning about innovations that were born out of everyday observations; these are the deepest of connections, a synthesis of the simple with the complex that is a form of higher thinking I truly admire.

Think about a disappointment you have experienced. What was your response?

Eat ice cream

Realize world has not ended

Practice situation to prepare myself for next disappointment

Challenge disappointment

Realize disappointment is not so disappointing when you enjoy the process more than you need the result.

Suite-style living may be an integral part of your Yale College experience. What would you contribute to the dynamic of your suite?

Punny jokes; endless supplies of Nutella and bacon; a funny but productive studying companion; a spontaneous exploration partner; "hipster" music; musicals in the shower; inspirational quotes from Neil DeGrasse Tyson; enthusiasm for any topic I am introduced to.

What do you wish you were better at being or doing?

With time, I can craft transcendent crescendos of language, words that tinkle both lyrically and emotionally, stories that move the most wooden layers of the soul; but ask me to speak them in public, and I sound like a wookiee.

THE ROAD TO YALE

Chapter

14

Olivia

PUBLIC HIGH SCHOOL
UNITED STATES

Public High School, U.S.

Freshman	Sophomore	Junior	Senior
English 9	Honors English 10	Honors English 11	AP English Literature
Honors Algebra II/ Trigonometry	High Honors Pre-Calculus	AP Calculus BC	Multivariable Calculus (MIT Open Courseware)
Honors French II	Honors French III	Honors French IV	AP French
World History I	World History II	AP U.S. History	AP Microeconomics
Honors Biology	Health	AP Computer Science	AP Physics C
Symphony Orchestra	Honors Chemistry	Honors Physics	Chamber Orchestra
	Chamber Orchestra	Chamber Orchestra	

Before High School and Outside Classes

Honors Geometry	Online AP Biology
Honors French I	Online AP Chemistry

Olivia

EXTRACURRICULAR AND WORK EXPERIENCE
All-girls a cappella group, Soprano 1 (11–12)
AP Calculus BC, Teaching assistant (11–12)
Columbia University Science Honors Program (11–12)
High school math team, President (9–12)
High school science bowl team, President (9–12)
National Honor Society, Tutor (11–12)
New York State Math League (10–11)
Piano (1–12)
Schools Helping Schools Club, President (10–12)
Science Olympiad Team, President (9–12)
Skiing, Junior varsity ski team (1–11)
Tennis (1–9)
Track, Varsity winter team (10–11)
U.S. State Department, Student ambassador (11–12)
Violinist, School string and chamber orchestras (3–12)

SUMMER ACTIVITIES
Garcia MRSEC Summer Research Program, Stony Brook University, NY (11)
U.S. State Department, East-West Center Partnership for Youth Program with Cambodia (10)
Columbia University, Engineering Design via Community Service Projects (10)
AwesomeMath summer program (9)
Center for Talented Youth, Johns Hopkins University, Probability and Game Theory (9)

AWARDS AND HONORS
Academics
Dartmouth Book Award (12)
National Merit Scholar (12)
NY State Math League Division B, Westchester County A Team, First Place (12)
AP Scholar with Distinction (11)
Bausch + Lomb Honorary Science Award, High school award (11)
Junior Academic Excellence Award (11)
Westchester County Math Team, Top 20 Individual (County), Top-35 Team (10–11)
Westchester County Meets, No. 1 Female High School Math Team (11)
Science Olympiad, Regional competition, First, Second, and Fourth Places (9–12)
Mandelbrot Competition, Best Freshman in School (9)

Service
Volunteer Service Award (11–12)

Arts
Concert Festival Competition, Baruch Performing Arts Center, Piano, First Place (10)
New York State School Music Association, Piano (10–11)

COMMON APPLICATION ESSAY

Some students have a background or story that is so central to their identity that they believe their application would be incomplete without it. If this sounds like you, then please share your story. (250-650 words)

Sitting in an ornate Cambodian temple, I had no idea how to react when a monk suddenly asked to be my Facebook friend. Not once did I ever expect that to happen. His genuine and accepting gaze stared down at me. His dark eyes expressed camaraderie and patience. I had always imagined that a monk would have a shaved head, a neon orange robe, bare feet, and a reserved demeanor. The funny thing was, his appearance lived up to my stereotype. But I never expected that a monk would ask to "friend" me.

"Sure," I blurted as I told him my name, which he quickly scribbled down.

I was sent to Cambodia by the U.S. State Department's East-West Center as President of my high school's Schools Helping Schools Club. My club had raised $11,000 to supply a clean water filtration tank to the Angprey Primary School. I was there to act as an American ambassador, teach English, and participate in the construction of the water tank. But out of curiosity, I stopped at a Buddhist temple nearby, where I happened to encounter a monk who was willing to chat with an inquisitive foreigner.

Before the monk's unanticipated request, I'd been talking to him about his life. I was impressed to learn that not only did he speak Khmer, but also he spoke English. I also learned that he wakes up daily at 4 am, and much of his day was filled with prayer, solitude, meditation, and the reading of Buddhist texts.

He buoyantly described his ascetic one or two meals a day, consisting of a bowl of rice and vegetables. Guilty feelings of gluttony crept into me, as one so coddled that I could eat all the cookies and pizzas I desired, surrounded by infinite food options. He recounted how his parents sent him to a monastery to get a better education and life. For all this, he willingly led a life of austerity and self-abnegation. Economically, he relied mostly on donations from the local people: nothing more, nothing less. I commended his self-discipline and ability to accept the simple life, never complaining or whining about his Spartan diet.

Somehow this meeting felt empowering, as if my values were being restored. I desired to emulate the monk, to experience his enlightened state. No, I don't mean I wanted to shave my head Britney Spears style and wear a fluorescent toga. Inspired by him, I wanted to challenge myself, become more selfless, and contribute in positive ways to the well-being of others.

And so once I left the monastery, I attempted to drop all my mental baggage and focused on the main goal of my trip: installing a water tank at a primary school in Takeo. I felt deeply honored to be the one supplying clean water to a community that truly needed it. As I worked alongside local residents digging ditches for pipes and assembling parts of the filter, a smile covered my sweaty, yet determined face.

Seeing how appreciative the community was, I suddenly became much more ambitious about serving others. I didn't want to provide only one community with a water tank but became driven to collect more money back home to donate water tanks to more communities around Takeo. With the new friendships and connections I formed with Cambodian monks and teachers, I chose their communities as future locations of water tanks. My new mission as President of the Schools Helping Schools Club was to raise as much money as possible to support as many people as possible. I loved the energy I derived from knowing I could tangibly help entire communities of people.

When I arrived back home after my trip and went on the computer, I smiled just thinking about my new Facebook friend, hoping to message him about my newfound optimism, my success in Takeo, and my enthusiasm for my new sense of mission.

SUPPLEMENTAL ESSAY

In this essay, please reflect on something you would like us to know about you that we might not learn from the rest of your application, or on something about which you would like to say more. You may write about anything—from personal experiences or interests to intellectual pursuits. (500 words or less)

For seven weeks, I found myself immobilized in a small, cramped room. Neither the stifling air nor the modest, wooden desk fazed me. Instead, I found myself mesmerized by enchanting computer models and Java programs, captivated by thousands of alluring lines of code. No, I wasn't confined to a prison; I was locked into an amazing, newfound experience.

This past summer, I pursued cutting-edge research at the Garcia Materials Research Science and Engineering Center at Stony Brook University. Although it was amazing to be able to explore any materials research topic I wanted, I felt that seven weeks would only be enough to touch to surface. My mission was to determine new ways to optimize the sun. Yes, we talk about harnessing this source of unlimited energy using solar cells, but our tools are still relatively primitive for such a modern society. In order to progress and multiply solar power usage, we'd need more efficient collectors of sunlight, made of less costly, yet-to-be developed materials like organic polymers.

Thus, my focus at Stony Brook consisted mostly of materials and polymers research. That said, I never actually touched any of these materials. Instead, I designed and manipulated materials through computer simulations, investigating them on the nano-scale, rather than working with actual specimens in the lab. I found this to be much safer, more efficient, and yielding of immediate results. Experiments that once might have taken weeks or even month to perform using actual materials could produce answers in a matter of hours through computer simulations. In fact, I've come to see computer models as the panacea for many of science's major environmental perils.

My research yielded exciting new results: In seven weeks I was able to discover new polymer configurations to enhance organic solar cell technology. My simulations showed the optimal internal morphology needed for efficient organic polymer solar cells and the structural parameters to achieve that. In the solar cells I designed, I found that a column structure would be optimal within the cell because the large fraction of nanofillers near the column would allow for effective charge transport, leading to greater energy efficiency.

Overall, my experiments revealed new and more effective morphologies and parameters that should be used in creating efficient organic solar cells and greater energy production. Ultimately, this provides a major stepping stone in polymer solar cell technology, and it makes solar cells more viable as alternative energy sources.

Having gotten an exciting taste of materials research, I'm eager to delve much deeper. I'm craving the opportunity to pursue longer-term research opportunities, as there's so much more I want to explore.

WHY YALE
What in particular about Yale has influenced your decision to apply?
(100 words or less)

As a committed conservationist who was sent by the U.S. State Department to install water tanks in Cambodia and is most passionate about clean water distribution, I'm attracted to Yale for its Environmental Studies major, its five-year joint program with the School of Forestry, courses like "Water Resource Management," and "Watershed Cycles and Processes," and the research of Professor Menachem Elimelech on the sustainable filtration of water. I'd utilize Yale's shopping period, sign up for Khmer lessons, and am lured by the residential college system. I'm drawn to Yale's Engineers without Borders, Student Environmental Coalition, and Undergraduate Energy Club.

ADDITIONAL QUESTIONS
What excites you intellectually, really?
The concept that lone individuals who are self-motivated and skilled can make a positive difference in the lives of entire communities, and that all people are empowered to make positive contributions; I find that most intellectually exciting.

Think about a disappointment you have experienced. What was your response?
Arriving in Cambodia to build a water tank at the Angprey Primary School and learning that the neighboring towns also lacked drinking water was devastating. I resolved to raise more funds back home to help supply more tanks for Cambodian communities.

Suite-style living may be an integral part of your Yale College experience. What would you contribute to the dynamic of your suite?
I'd contribute piano accompaniment for those who share my passion for bursting out in song, DIY fix-it skills if anything breaks in the dorm, excellent study habits with enough to share, and lots of positive energy. Anyone want tap dance lessons?

What do you wish you were better at being or doing?
I'd love to speak Khmer, which I was exposed to in Cambodia, and Vietnamese (and would plan to enroll in Yale's Center for Language Study); Yale is one of the few universities to offer on-campus Vietnamese classes and Khmer through distance learning.

THE ROAD TO YALE

Chapter

15

Sato

PUBLIC HIGH SCHOOL
UNITED STATES

Public High School, U.S.

Freshman	Sophomore	Junior	Senior
Honor English 9	Honor English 10	AP English Language	AP English Literature
Honor Algebra II	Honor Pre-Calculus	AP Calculus AB	AP Calculus BC
Honor Biology	AP U.S. History	AP Chemistry	AP Physics C
Modern World History	Honor Chemistry	AP Euro History	AP U.S. Government & AP Macroeconomics
Spanish II	Programming I and II	AP Art Drawing	AP Art 2D
Drawing and Painting I	Drawing and Painting III	Honor Physics	Symphony Orchestra
Symphony Orchestra	Symphony Orchestra	Symphony Orchestra	Teacher Assistant
	Chinese I	Chinese II	Chinese III

Before High School and Outside Classes

Honors Geometry	Summer Health
Spanish I	

Sato

EXTRACURRICULAR AND WORK EXPERIENCE

Anderson's Test Kitchens Club, Co-founder (11–12)

Hackathon, Team organizer (11–12)

High school chamber and symphony orchestra, First violin (9–12)

Junior Engineering Technical Society, Science and math team leader (10–12)

Metro Art Academy, Youth artist project leader, community art festival host, Art Council (9–12)

Origami artist (9–12)

Ultimate Frisbee Club, Founder (11–12)

Varsity tennis, Co-captain (9–12)

Volunteer musician, art activist, volunteer tutor (9–12)

SUMMER ACTIVITIES

Stanford Summer College, Computer engineering (11)

Varsity tennis camp (10)

AWARDS AND HONORS

Academic

National Honor Society (12)

Cum Laude Society (12)

National Merit Scholarship Program, Semifinalist (12)

AP Scholar with Distinction (11)

Junior Engineering Technical Society, Junior Division, Third Place (11)

Junior Engineering Technical Society, Sophomore Division, First Place (10)

Teacher's Choice Award (9)

Arts

Scholastic Art & Writing Awards, Art and Painting, Gold Key (11–12)

Violin, First violin; State festivals, Top marks; National festival, Second place; Carnegie Hall performance (9–12)

Regional art awards (9–11)

Athletics

Varsity tennis, Most Improved Player Award (10)

Top Scholar Varsity Athlete Award (9–11)

COMMON APPLICATION ESSAY

Some students have a background or story that is so central to their identity that they believe their application would be incomplete without it. If this sounds like you, then please share your story. (250-650 words)

The Origami Kid

The room was dim and the video feed blurry, but the friendly voice was clear over Skype, "Hi, I'm Naomiki Sato." When the camera focused, I saw the face of a man with a broad smile. Mr. Sato, a well-known origami artist in Paris, France, had offered to give me a hands-on lesson after I asked him about his intricately-folded roses featured on a popular forum.

My fascination with origami started as a coping mechanism for geometry in middle school. I was bad at geometry, and I hated it. It was rugged territory where I could not help but fall on my face. Yet, I was proud and thought there was such a thing as a stupid question, so I did not ask for help. Instead, folding became my form of therapy. I didn't know then that the layers of folded paper would ultimately lead me to my best teacher.

Whether I was content or frustrated, paper was always there for me. I could manipulate it into elegant or grotesque forms to inspire a little more spirit. My world became one where everything could be creased, uncreased, folded, turned inside-out and folded again. Every day, I waded through a marsh of experimental models and wrinkled tessellations that had earned an "uhhh, what is it?" from my parents. But I couldn't have been more pleased, because through this exhausting process, I was creating things of my own. And yet I was not sated. Having the power to shape a simple piece of paper always reminded me of pushing forward the frontier of innovation.

When I came to a bit of unreadable diagram, I would move to video. When the videos became unwatchable, I read step-by-steps. When I could no longer bear the sight of words, I folded out of intuition. On one particularly perplexing figure, a fivefold rose, I reached an impasse. No matter how many times I folded and started over again, the paper would tear, along with my pride. I simply could not grasp the organic shape of the model. Eventually I became more afraid of not knowing than of asking for help. I hesitantly reached out to the model's designer, Naomiki Sato.

I did not expect a reply, but still I waited, stubbornly, enthusiastically, and secretly desperate for a response. Just as I had lost hope, and though he did not know me, Mr. Sato wrote back and offered to teach me. It wasn't so scary talking to him about more than just folding the model. We ended up chatting about music and cheeses, in addition to the creative process and the math behind the model. The same math later pushed me to overcome my hurdles in geometry and succeed in algebra II and pre-calculus.

Despite being separated by a generation and an ocean, we connected right away through our love for the art of origami. A few weeks later I received a package from Mr. Sato, inside was a handwritten note and a neatly packed origami rose—I instantly recognized it was the one we made together. Holding the rose in my hand, for the first time I realized that it took courage to ask for help, and when I did, the reward was more than I ever expected.

As years went by, I transitioned from middle school to high school and grew from unsure to confident. Nowadays, I often reflect on my friendship with Mr. Sato and how it has helped to shape me into a better thinker and problem solver. Maybe it was by chance that our paths crossed, or maybe it wasn't. I feel fortunate to be who I am today, always curious and persistent, ready to embrace the next leg of my journey.

SUPPLEMENTAL ESSAY
In this essay, please reflect on something you would like us to know about you that we might not learn from the rest of your application, or on something about which you would like to say more. You may write about anything—from personal experiences or interests to intellectual pursuits. (500 words or less)

The warm sound of live jazz, and the smell of spiced chili, a local favorite, permeated the air. Waves of people rose and receded in the ocean of small vendors and floating chit-chat—this was CliftonFest, an annual arts and music event that always draws a large crowd from near and far. As a community youth artist, I was hosting its "famous" sidewalk mural project. Along with a dozen other artists, I was about to create colorful chalk murals that would liven up public space throughout the neighborhood of Clifton, Ohio.

It was the absolute best time to meet friends, old and new, and show off my passion; people moved about the streets throughout the day, gathering around my artwork, and conversing with me while I was hunched over, working. Stroke by stroke, my work began to take shape—a seascape inspired by Impressionism and ukiyo-e, my two favorite art styles. "Fantastic work!" said Jan Checco, my mentor and a longtime local artist, as she stopped by to give her feedback and was very pleased to see how my piece coming together.

Creative art has always been one of my primary activities outside of classroom and the most important to my intellectual growth. In addition to taking art class grade 9 through 12, over the years I have enrolled in summer and weekend art studios from Cincinnati Art Academy, become a youth art apprentice working under local artists, and participated in various community based art projects.

Art is a vital part of the human existence. I love art not only because it is a means for self-expression, but also a versatile platform for cultivating my creativity in all realms. In my free time, you may find me folding intricate origami out of a piece of paper, finishing off my matcha creme brûlée with a perfectly formed golden sugar-crust, or tactfully stuffing wires into an already-full breadboard. In the future, I'd like this same fascination to mature; I can see myself designing both visually organic and functional exoskeletons for people with limited mobility, or perhaps creating a new program to help improve productivity through simplicity and intuitiveness. I love creating things, and in whatever path I take in the future, the artist in me always guides me every step of the way.

WHY YALE?

What in particular about Yale has influenced your decision to apply?
(100 words or less)

The happy students, residential college life, outstanding academic programs, robust spirit of volunteerism, diverse community and close-knit network of students and faculty are just a few things I've learned about Yale. On top of that I am particularly drawn to the vibrant art culture at Yale, which is fully evidenced by the events listed on Yale Art Calendar, with its impressive artistic breadth and depth. I plan to be an integral link of the rich arts and cultural tradition at Yale, immersing myself in its numerous creative offerings, and actively participating in its various community outreach programs.

ADDITIONAL QUESTIONS

What excites you intellectually, really?
For me, engineering and design go hand-in-hand like Camembert and cranberry jam; there's nothing quite so satisfying as exploring the slightly nutty calculations that complement the refreshing tartness of a well-designed project.

Think about a disappointment you have experienced. What was your response?
At the end of Stanford Summer College, I missed the picture with my very close-knit group of friends due to needing to spend time in the electronics lab. Though I later had the chance to say bye to all my friends, I really wish I was in that picture.

Suite-style living may be an integral part of your Yale College experience. What would you contribute to the dynamic of your suite?
My wit and quirky creativity. I'm known for my snarky jokes during board games and movies, my shower song covers and failed baking experiments.

What do you wish you were better at being or doing?
Definitely a better guitar player! I have been playing violin for 12 years, but always thought being a high-caliber guitar player would be cooler. Don't worry, I don't play Wonderwall.

THE ROAD TO YALE

Chapter

16

Sophia

PRIVATE HIGH SCHOOL
CANADA

Private High School, Canada

Freshman*	Sophomore*	Junior	Senior
English 9	English 10	English 11	English 12
Principles of Mathematics 10	Introduction to Functions	Advanced Functions	AP Calculus AB/ Vectors
Geography	Introduction to Computer Science	Computer Science	AP Physics 1
French 9	French 10	French 11	French 12
Science 10	Biology 11	AP Biology	Data Management/ Statistics
Latin I	Chemistry 11	AP Chemistry	Economics
Spanish I	American History	Physics 11	World History
Civics/History	Career Studies	PE	
Visual Arts	PE		
PE			

Before High School and Outside Classes

Principles of Mathematics 9

Canadian History

Science 9

* Some classes are one-semester classes.

Sophia

EXTRACURRICULAR AND WORK EXPERIENCE

Canadian Biology Olympiad (10-12)

Community service and programs for developmentally disabled, Program assistant, camp counselor, classroom assistant (7-12)

DECA, Competitor (10-11)

Gymnastics, Competitor (4-12)

HOSA, Co-president and co-founder (11-12)

SUMMER ACTIVITIES

Local university, Research assistant (11)

Jr. DEEP Summer Academy Entrepreneurship and Engineering program, Shad Valley, Camp counselor (10)

Gymnastics, Summer training (9)

National math camp (9)

DEEP Summer Academy, University of Toronto (8)

AWARDS AND HONORS

Duke of Edinburgh Gold Award (11)

International Career Development Conference, First Place (11)

Michael Smith Science Challenge, Second Place (National) (11)

North American Computational Linguistics Olympiad, Sixth Place (National) (11)

Provincial Youth Service Award (11)

Beaver Computing Competition, First Place (10)

Cayley Math Contest, First Place (10)

World Challenge Cup, Aesthetic Group Gymnastics, Tenth Place (International Debut) (9)

National Biology Scholar (10-11)

Provincial Championships and Eastern Canadian Championships, Rhythmic Gymnastics, Top 2 finishes (9-11)

COMMON APPLICATION ESSAY

Some students have a background or story so central to their identity that they believe their application would be incomplete without it. Share this story. (250–650 words)

The ribbon lands softly on my legs as my music draws to a close. After 9 years in rhythmic gymnastics, the ribbon has become my fifth limb, and the flowing spirals it forms are as fundamental to me as the helices of my DNA. My gym has become my second home; my coach has become my second mother and my teammates have become my sisters. Although we compete against each other, we never hesitate to help each other learn new throws or pivots, recognizing that we can build off of each other's strengths to achieve greater heights. It is a calming atmosphere, a place where everyone has bonded over the same goals of sliding a few inches lower in over-split, or doing a few more sit-ups. While at the gym, I can let go of all of my worries and stress, and instead, focus on the energy I feel radiating through my ribbon every time I pick it up.

It has not always been this way though. When I first started gymnastics at age 8, my ribbon did not dance but instead lay limply at my feet. Compared to the other girls, I was chubbier and less flexible. Doubt that I could succeed and fear of being judged crept into my mind. As I looked around at all of my astonishingly flexible and lithe teammates, I began to feel like a tree stump in a bamboo forest. Every day I would suck in my stomach to see if it had gotten any flatter and pull my leg up to see if it could go any higher. As a young girl overwhelmed with the long training sessions, unfamiliar environment, and pressure to lose weight, I briefly considered quitting. But something about the way the loops of my ribbon lay on the floor told of intriguing potential to be uncovered only with time.

Over years of sweat and tears in the gym, my ribbon slowly came alive. It is the same length of rayon as anyone else's, just like each person's DNA is made up of the same nucleotides. However, as I learned its secrets, my ribbon became uniquely mine and its movements reflect my personality, from my smooth and methodical triple-chaînés-walkover risk to my quirky side-tilt balance into side wave. Each of these elements took me many long hours to learn, and the first time I perfected each brought me immense satisfaction, knowing that all of my hard work paid off.

When I feel drained from stress at school or at home, I know that once I get to the gym, I will find my ribbon waiting for me. Every time the music for my routine plays, the outside world falls away. Together, my ribbon and I create a new fantasy world and invite others in with our movements. Long after the music ends, a little piece of that world stays in my heart and creeps into everything I do. Like my ribbon soaring through the air, I constantly seek new adventures. Remembering how I deftly recover after mistakes during competitions, I have learned to think on my feet, and the roles my coach and teammates have played in helping me uncover my ribbon's potential have inspired a drive in me to do the same for others through coaching younger gymnasts and passing on my knowledge.

Today, the spark of possibility I saw in my once lifeless ribbon has grown into an emotional home for me within the haven of my gym. At the same time, I know that it will fall to the ground once again, unless I keep it moving through new challenges and adventures. But I know that I will. Armed with the ribbons of my DNA, nothing can stop me.

SUPPLEMENTAL ESSAY

In this essay, please reflect on something you would like us to know about you that we might not learn from the rest of your application, or on something about which you would like to say more. You may write about anything—from personal experiences or interests to intellectual pursuits. (500 words or less)

People say that time is money. Indeed, it is as if we begin each day with a fat paycheck that slowly dwindles away with each second. Spent wisely, each paycheck can be converted into meaningful experiences that ultimately help us grow. But if we are not careful in budgeting, we may find ourselves with maxed out credit cards at the end of each day, living paycheck to paycheck without the chance to do everything that we wanted.

I learned this the hard way. One weekend, I found myself with a schedule that was more packed than usual. Saturday morning, I had gymnastics practice. Afterwards, I had a meeting with a Carnival Cruise Lines customer service representative for my DECA project. Later in the afternoon, I staked out craft stores around the city for white ribbon so that the Gender Equity Committee could run the White Ribbon Campaign.

Finally, that night I volunteered at the Canada-China Cultural Development Association's 7th Anniversary Celebration. Upon finally returning home, exhausted, I realized that I had failed to budget time for a good night's rest before a gymnastics competition the next day. Unsurprisingly, I did not perform well.

The disappointment I experienced after that competition made me consider how I could have done things differently. It forced me to reflect on whether I was using my time in the best way possible. It gave me a deeper understanding of what I value. While time only moves forward and there is no point in trying to change the past, I endeavored to use my new insights to become a better investor of time in the future.

I thought about the refreshing sense of peace I gain from gymnastics practice. I thought about the pride I feel every time a developmentally delayed student who I volunteer with learns how to cook a new dish. I thought about how empowered I had felt after completing my Canadian Biology Olympiad portfolio despite my many unexpected challenges (including designing my own labs and having to run to Shoppers Drug Mart for ethanol when the supply at my school was depleted). With a new-found understanding of my priorities, I began to make a conscious effort to spend my time wisely. When penciling in my schedule, activities and tasks that I consider important take precedent over those I simply consider urgent. It is difficult to reallocate time away from activities that I have been committed to for many years such as DECA. But doing so allows me to dedicate more time to those I care about the most.

Everything I wish to do, see, experience, and accomplish can only fit into the time I am given. Yet I am still ultimately the one in control, as I have the ability to invest this time in ways that reflect what I value. After all, as Michael Altshuler said, "The bad news is time flies. The good news is you're the pilot."

WHY YALE
What in particular about Yale has influenced your decision to apply?
(100 words or less)

"Do you need any help?" After watching me wander around staring at my map, a concerned student approached me. It was just one of many encounters that convinced me that while Yale offers an incredible residential college system and undergraduate focus in a research institution (the fact that all tenured professors teach undergraduates is a testament to this), one of its greatest assets is the welcoming Yale community. It is incredible seeing so many talented individuals come together in a community where everyone can learn from each other's perspectives to become even greater.

ADDITIONAL QUESTIONS
What excites you intellectually, really?
I used to think scientists were godlike prodigies. However, after completing my portfolio for the Canadian Biology Olympiad, I realized that I could use my skills to make a personal contribution to scientific knowledge. I was hooked.

Think about a disappointment you have experienced. What was your response?
After a year of hard work, my partner and I failed to qualify for the International Development Conference 2013 by a single point. But there were no tears or finger-pointing—only determination to use what we had learned to do better in 2014.

Suite-style living—four to six students sharing a set of rooms—may be an integral part of your Yale College experience. What would you contribute to the dynamic of your suite?
Greetings suitemates! To find me, just look for a perpetually smiling face or someone doing euphoric leprechaun jumps down the hall. I will be your running buddy and your shoulder to cry on, your fellow plant enthusiast and your partner-in-crime.

What do you wish you were better at being/doing?
Usually people who love food are good at cooking. I am not the usual. When I attempt to bake delicious cookies, I find myself with a pan full of rocks. Until I improve, I must team up with friends skilled at cooking to form cooking-tasting teams.

THE ROAD TO YALE

Chapter

17

Steven

PUBLIC HIGH SCHOOL
UNITED STATES

Public High School, U.S.

Freshman*	Sophomore*	Junior	Senior
Algebra II	Computer Integrated Manufacturing	AP Calculus	AP Physics C
Biology	Data Analysis 2	AP Chemistry	AP Statistics
Data Analysis I	English 2	English 3	English 4
English I	Guidance	Health 3	Multivariable Calculus
Guidance	Health 2	Spanish 4	Spanish Conversation and Composition
Health I	Physics	U.S. History 2	
Intro to Engineering Design	Pre-Calculus		
Intro to Research	Principles of Engineering		
Software Applications	Research Practicum		
Spanish 2	Spanish 3		
World History	U.S. History 1		

* Some classes are one-semester classes.

Steven

EXTRACURRICULARS AND WORK EXPERIENCE

American Computer Science League (11-12)
Class Council, Student government representative (10-12)
Experimental Research Club (10-12)
International Flavors and Fragrances Internship (12)
Riverview Medical Center, Volunteer (9-10)
Special People United to Ride Program, Volunteer (10-11)
Student Government Executive Council, School officer (11-12)
Technology Student Association, State officer (9-12)
Tennis, USTA tournament competitor (2-12)
Varsity tennis, Captain (9-12)

SUMMER ACTIVITIES

Private tennis instructor (11-12)
Rockefeller University, Research intern (11)
Henry Ford Health System, Research intern (10)
Stony Brook University Biotechnology, Research summer program (10)

AWARDS AND HONORS

Academics
Academy of Arts and Sciences, Annual National Meeting (12)
National Merit, Finalist (12)
Mathematical Contest for Modeling (12)
Annual High School International Mathematical Contest for Modeling,
   Outstanding Paper (Highest Award Given to Top 8 Papers) (12)
Siemens Award for Advanced Placement State Winner (11)
Technology Student Association National Conference Biotechnology,
   First Place (11)
American Junior Academy of Science, Biochemistry Research Lifetime Fellow (11)
Design Competition (11)
United States National Chemistry Olympiad, Semifinalist (11)
United States National Physics Olympiad, Semifinalist (10)

Athletics
1st Singles County Tennis Tournament Champion (11)
All-Conference Tennis Player of the Year (11)
USTA National Zone Team 16's Championships Finalist Team (10)
United States Tennis Association, National Tournament Doubles Champion (9)

COMMON APPLICATION ESSAY
Topic of your choice. (250-650 words)

My First Beauty Pageant

Time was running out. It was almost my turn, but the rose in my shaking hands was still adorned with its leaves. But why was I nervous at all? My hours of preparation had certainly been adequate. After fumbling the rose for a few more seconds, I was finally able to strip off the sinewy leaves. Deep breath. As the entrance to the auditorium drifted closer, my mind swelled with questions and answers:

"How embarrassing will this be?"

"I can't let my friends and their families down; I promised them a show."

My thoughts were suddenly cut short by the onset of the song that I had selected to walk to: "Listen to Your Heart" by DHT. I fluttered down the runway, letting the spotted wings on my back dissipate the worries away with each flap. Immediately, the audience roared with laughter and cheered, showing its appreciation of my peculiar outfit: a black button-down shirt to complement black jeans, topped off with red shutter shades, a fitted Superman cap, and a pair of ladybug wings borrowed from my best friend's little sister. High school paparazzi, or overenthusiastic yearbook club members, followed in chase as I leaped and twirled, slowly surrendering to my Coccinellidae magnifica insect alter-ego. Onwards, I pranced down the runway amidst a flashing array of dizzying lights. My torso twisted and my feet glided as if following some dainty choreography until at last, I delivered my rose — the final touch — to my history teacher at the judges' table. Then, I assumed a fierce akimbo pose worthy of an appearance on America's Next Top Model. As the crowd's growing energy spread around the room, my mouth gradually turned into a grin, betraying my affected model demeanor.

I was flooded with giddy joy when the MC announced that the audience had voted me through to the final round to showcase a talent. Donning a basketball jersey, I performed a rendition of Lebron James's pregame ritual (substituting baby powder for Lebron's usual chalk powder) before demonstrating my honed athletic abilities with a round of cup-stacking. Rap music blared in the background as I cup-stacked vigorously, riding a wave of my friends' cheers through the complete cycle stack sequence.

Noticing my Spanish instructor smiling with her children when I hit the runway and the judges holding their faces in laughter when I turned the corner are unforgettable moments. A snapshot of the energized audience during the cup-stacking remains etched in my memory. Although I did not win the "Mr. — High School" title, I was deeply humbled by my supporters who contributed to my fundraising basket. Through my first beauty pageant, I discovered how enjoyable it is to bring happiness to others both near and far.

The following day, Mrs. M greeted me in the school hallway: "Hey there, guess what's in a vase sitting on my kitchen table." I thought about the rose and smiled.

SUPPLEMENTAL ESSAY
Yale Engineering Essay (500 words or less)

Since my childhood, my fascination with creation and the applied sciences has evolved from filling my house with Lego models to enrolling in a specialized engineering school. I have always loved solving problems with a hands-on approach. But my enthusiasm reached a new high when I was exposed to the engineering feats in premier science research laboratories.

Two summers ago, I stepped into the Henry Ford Health System labs to research an inhibitor of age-related macular degeneration. When my mentor introduced me to the fluorescence microscope, fundus photography hardware, incubators, and other machines around the lab, I was captivated by the technology; these elegant machines would take an input of data and consequently output some magical, technical prose. I challenged myself to learn as much as possible about the technology around the lab. Accordingly, I spent much of my time there earnestly questioning my mentor and the post-doctorate fellows about the high resolution photography, the microscope's mechanisms for filtering ultraviolet light, and the methods to quantify a seemingly qualitative variable: vascularization.

The next summer, as a research intern at The Rockefeller University, I implemented an intricate experimental setup and finalized a blockface imaging protocol to digitally reconstruct liver vasculature. My setup consisted of Thorlab anti-vibration breadboards, Phidget motion sensors, Peltier devices, an automated microtome head, and numerous circuit boards and wires strewn all over. It was fascinating to see such diverse components join together to perform wholly new functions. I finally experienced the less polished side of engineering, yet more than ever, I was able to appreciate the raw beauty of creation and the vast applications of different branches of science.

My experiences have led me to the realization that engineers create change. Behind every professional, there is an invention, an innovation, an engineer. Yale's engineering program offers a liberal arts curriculum that establishes a solid foundation of analytical and critical thinking skills. In addition, it provides an understanding of the complex social, political, economic, and environmental issues that come with new technological products and processes. Through the School of Engineering and Applied Science, I will be able to further develop an interdisciplinary approach to problem solving by immersing myself in Yale's intellectual, collaborative atmosphere.

Through my studies of chemical engineering at Yale, I would have the chance to work closely with world class faculty both in the classroom and in the laboratory. The low student-faculty ratio in the engineering department would allow me to learn directly from some of the brightest minds in their respective fields. Moreover, the abundance of undergraduate research opportunities would further supplement my learning, whether it is through working towards developing a novel targeted therapy process or studying drug design and pharmaceutical formulations. I would love to channel my knowledge and creativity into creation on the molecular level, and I truly believe that Yale engineering will help guide me in my pursuit of innovation. Engineers are practical dreamers, and I look forward to one day sharing my dreams with the world.

WHY YALE?

What in particular about Yale has influenced your decision to apply?
(100 words or less)

Besides the unique residential colleges, beautiful landscaping, and friendly atmosphere, Yale offers an exceptional academic program full of resources in every field. Coming from the pre-engineering high school, I would love to be able to expand on my interests in the humanities while pursuing my passion for engineering. Yale's curriculum integrates different disciplines while allowing flexibility in exploring new areas. Even the motto — "Light and Truth" — attracts my scientific side.

ADDITIONAL QUESTIONS

What would you do with a free afternoon tomorrow?
I would really like to go on a hot-air balloon ride and see things from a new perspective.

What is the best piece of advice you have received in the last three years?
"Just dreaming is not enough; you need determination and hard work to achieve your dreams." —My Grandfather

If you could witness one moment in history, what would it be and why?
I would like to observe Sir Ernest Rutherford's working apparatus for his gold foil experiment, due to my interests in chemistry, physics, and research.

What do you wish you were better at being or doing?
I wish I could sing better. There is something so inspiring and moving about a beautiful voice.

What is something about which you have changed your mind in the last three years?
I have always gravitated towards math and science, but over the past few years I have come to appreciate the value of the humanities and writing in particular.

THE ROAD TO YALE

Chapter

18

Vivian

**PUBLIC HIGH SCHOOL
UNITED STATES**

Public High School, U.S.

Freshman	Sophomore	Junior	Senior
Honors English I	Honors English II	AP English Language	AP English Literature
Honors Geometry	Honors Algebra II	Honors Pre-Calculus	AP Statistics
Honors Biology	Honors Chemistry	AP Chemistry	AP Calculus BC
Honors World Geography	AP World History	AP U.S. History	AP U.S. Government and AP Macroeconomics
Honors Spanish II	Honors Spanish III	Honors Physics	AP Spanish Literature IV
AP Music Theory	Honors Computer Science	AP Human Geography	AP Biology
Tennis	Tennis	Honors and AP Psychology	Teacher's Assistant

Before High School and Outside Classes

Honors Algebra I	Honors Spanish I

Vivian

EXTRACURRICULAR AND WORK EXPERIENCE

Dance, Solo and team dancer (K–12)
Disaster relief and community service organization, Co-founder (5–12)
Habitat for Humanity Club, President and co-founder (11–12)
Interact Club, Secretary (11–12)
State Poetry Society, Member and competitor (9–12)
Tennis (6–10)
Writing, Competitor and blogger (3–12)
Youth Service America Global Youth Council (12)

SUMMER ACTIVITIES

Stony Brook University, Simons summer research fellow (11)
Methodist Hospital, Research intern (10)
English workshop, China, Organizer (9)

AWARDS AND HONORS

Academic
Journal of American Chemistry Society, Co-author (11)
State Poetry Society's A Book of The Year, Published poems (11)
State Poetry Society, First Place (High School Award) (11)
Nestlé Very Best In Youth, National Finalist (10)
"It's All Write" short story writing contest, Ann Arbor Library, Finalist (10)
Scholastic Art & Writing Awards, Poetry Collection, Gold Key (7–8, 11–12)
Scholastic Art & Writing Awards, Science Fiction/Fantasy, Silver Key (10–11)

Service
National Society of High School Scholars, Robert Sheppard Leadership Award (11)
Congressional Award, Silver and Gold Medals (10–11)
Youth Service America and Disney, Radio Disney Hero for Change Award (10)
GenerationOn Excellence in Service and Leadership Award (10)
President's Volunteer Service Award, Gold (9–11)
MSN 16 Incredible Kids Who Are Saving the World (9)

Performing Arts
StarQuest Performing Arts International, Regional Competition, First Place Overall,
  Distinctive Award "Beautiful Shapes" (11)
Showstopper Mid-America, National Finals Competition, Second Place Overall, First
  Place Senior Division, Folkloric Solo (10)
Showstopper American Dance Championships, Regional Competition, Seventh
  Place Overall, First Place Teen Division, Folkloric Solo (10)

Athletics
Girls' Doubles Varsity Division B, Regional invitation tournament, Second Place (10)
Girls' Single Freshmen Division B, Regional tournament, First Place (9)

COMMON APPLICATION ESSAY

Some students have a background or story so central to their identity that they believe their application would be incomplete without it. Share this story. (250–650 words)

Coming into Focus

Last year, I stood in front of my lab bench, squinting into a microscope. I adjusted the focus and watched the cells blur into razor-edged sharpness. For the next three hours, I continued to transfer cells onto the slide.

At the time, I didn't realize it, but now I know; this is how history begins. We like to think of discoveries in terms of white-haired men waving bubbling beakers, but in real life it is less of a caricature. Somehow, it is just as rewarding.

Discovery is a process, one that found me on a stool in my biomedical engineering lab, latex gloves stretched taut across my palms and a name tag clipped to my crinkled white lab coat, falling in love with science and all that it meant. Research has shown me that biology isn't just regurgitating definitions. It's questioning, experimenting, and making discoveries.

I was working on a pipet to isolate single cells. The technology is the first of its kind, and it vastly benefits researchers in all fields, whether they're running single cell polymerase chain reactions or conducting clone selection experiments. But perhaps most importantly, this novel technique provides a new avenue for the study of cancer cell heterogeneity. The thought that the technology I was working on could impact research in so many different fields was astonishing, but it was even more incredible to think that my contribution, however slight, could help fight the disease that my grandmother had died from and my parents have spent a lifetime studying.

The thrill of experimentation, of being part of a breakthrough, is truly unparalleled. Whether it's sequencing the human genome or understanding the cell cycle, every discovery in science has applications in the real world, a world that extends beyond test tubes and beakers and the sterile, beautiful environment that comes to life under latex gloves and laboratory goggles.

I want to be someone who is changing the world, who is finding the cure, who is asking the questions, the same questions I can't stop myself from asking now. But that's not who I want to be ten years from now. That's who I want to be today.

I used to think that making discoveries meant men in white lab coats, running into crowded rooms announcing their breakthroughs, I now know that it can also be so much more. It can be working at a lab bench, pipetting cells for hours, and watching the world shift into focus through the lens of a microscope.

SUPPLEMENTAL ESSAY

In this essay, please reflect on something you would like us to know about you that we might not learn from the rest of your application, or on something about which you would like to say more. You may write about anything—from personal experiences or interests to intellectual pursuits. (500 words or less)

First Love

The first notes lilt by and my eyes drift shut as I take in a deep breath, tasting the electricity in the air and the rich texture of the music. There is an intimacy that engulfs me in every note; God knows how many times I ran that track over and over again, getting lost in the harmony even when my little brother yelled at me to turn it off.

The stage feels hollow beneath me as I rise to the balls of my feet.

I saw myself standing on the stage in Manhattan at age three, nose red from the crisp winter wind and in a pink tutu and tights, beaming brighter than the twinkling lights in our Christmas recital...

And breathe. I exhale sharply, drawing my fingers in a smooth arc to my right and letting the swell and crash of the song guide me.

But after moving to Texas, things had gotten hectic and my love for dance seemed to ebb. The tightly woven community of this new dance class did not include me, and the instructors and I were not familiar with one another. I stopped wanting to go and it became more my parents' coercion that got me to practice each week rather than my own willpower.

My foot slips a quarter inch across the stage and my heart speeds up as I regain my footing.

Then at one of our biannual performances, just as the music had begun to play, I found myself crammed in the very back row. I paused for a split second, letting the melody slip from my grasp as I wondered where the passionate little girl had gone—the one who fought to perfect every pirouette and arabesque, even if just for a warmup.

I'd gone so long just barely getting by that I hadn't stopped to see who I'd become. That not giving 100% wasn't who I was and never would be. And I realized that the girl I used to be was still there—if I could just let her.

The spotlight embraces me and in mid plié, my eyes to wash over the audience. I can just barely make out the judges sitting in the front row.

I came back not as someone who just did the movements but as a dancer who was committed to perform them.

A cell phone rings in the distance but the tide has already taken me by storm.

Weeks blurred into months as I gave it my all. I sought help again and again from students and teachers alike, and hours after the last dancer had gone home I'd still be left standing in the studio, hair plastered to my face with sweat, striving to perfect every breath.

I soar across the stage, willing my fingertips to kiss the curtains as I hold my breath and the music crescendos, sending a current of exhilaration down my spine.

Two years later, my dance instructor moved me to the first row for our upcoming performance and I cried.

I am untouchable.

I'd dreamed of it for so long. Not because of the status it represented, but to again remember the enthralled faces of the audience and the blazing white of the lights, rather than the backs of the dancers as I hid myself.

Because the front row wasn't just the costumes and the spotlights and the rolling applause. It was the long hours and late nights of practice—it was seeing months and years of hard work pay off.

I spin across the stage in a whirlwind, hands slicing through the air and head whipping as the world and I spiral into one.

I never did forget the love that I felt for every breath I took in when I danced...

The love that I still feel now.

And as the melody fades to silence, standing on the stage at Nationals and fighting to catch my breath with the audience rising to their feet, I wonder how I could have ever forgotten...

My first love.

WHY YALE

What in particular about Yale has influenced your decision to apply?
(100 words or less)

From science to service, Yale gives me the opportunity to advance my passions. Its shopping period lets me create my own experience in biology, whether through the Department of MCDB or the Department of Biomedical Engineering. And when 95% of undergraduate science majors research with faculty, it's clear that Yale develops students with incredible caliber. But not just in their academics, my love for community service can be met with student organizations like The Leadership Institute and the Global China Connection.

I have many passions but only Yale allows me to pursue them all and still discover new interests.

ADDITIONAL QUESTIONS

What excites you intellectually, really?
In 1,000 years, I'll cease to exist but my DNA could live on through the infinite growth of cancer cells. Although frightening, it's fascinating that the key to immortality may be behind the door that accounts for a fourth of our nation's deaths.

Think about a disappointment you have experienced. What was your response?
I started community service when I was ten and received comments of "shouldn't you let the grown-ups handle this?" But I continued on, not only for the victims of disaster but to raise awareness for service and the power of youth.

Suite-style living may be an integral part of your Yale College experience. What would you contribute to the dynamic of your suite?
I'm a middle child, so I've always ended up solving problems. That also means I have to keep a level head. Plus, as someone passionate about both STEM and the humanities, I can see both sides of an issue, whether it's personal or academic.

What do you wish you were better at being or doing?
I wish I were better at making snap decisions. I have a habit of making a list of pros and cons, which can unnecessarily prolong the decision-making process.

THE ROAD TO YALE

Acknowledgments

We owe a debt of gratitude to all of the authors who contributed their application materials to the book, without whom this project would not have been possible. We are also grateful to the parents of the authors, who helped collect materials, offered ideas on the development of the book, and promoted the online version of this publication. In particular, we thank Yiping Guo and Hong Zhou for their invaluable ideas and helpful discussions during the making of *The Road to Yale.*

Many thanks to Wendy Peng for publishing *The Road to Yale* online at www.theprimetutor.com. For more information and for updates on the book, please visit The PrimeTutor's website. Julia Guo, director of VSA Future, was a great help in the production of the book. For more advice and guidance on college counseling, visit www.vsafuture.com.